D0481909

The Man
Who Broke
Purple

The Life of
Colonel William F. Friedman,
Who Deciphered the Japanese Code
in World War II

The Man
Who Broke
Purple

The Life of
Colonel William F. Friedman,
Who Deciphered the Japanese Code
in World War II

by Ronald Clark

Little, Brown and Company   Boston   Toronto

FIRST AMERICAN EDITION

T 09/77

Library of Congress Cataloging in Publication Data

Clark, Ronald William.
   The man who broke Purple.

   Includes index.
   1. Friedman, William Frederick, 1891–1969.
   2. Cryptographers—United States—Biography.
   I. Title.
   UB290.C58 1977 358'.24 [B] 77–10004
   ISBN 0–316–14595–5

Designed by Christine Benders

PRINTED IN THE UNITED STATES OF AMERICA

Contents

Unless otherwise noted, the photographs are from the personal collection of Mrs. William Friedman.

Acknowledgments

The author wishes to thank Mrs. Elizebeth Friedman and the members of her family for their generous help and cooperation and for their permission to quote from the late Colonel Friedman's writings. The author is also grateful for the help, hospitality and cooperation of the staff of the George C. Marshall Foundation of Lexington, Virginia, and for the help of others in the United States, Europe and Japan. However, he alone is responsible for the material used — much of it from sources other than those identified above — and for the opinions expressed.

The author wishes to thank the Trustees of the Estate of Nelle Fabyan for permission to quote letters of the late Colonel Fabyan.

The Man
Who Broke
Purple

The Life of
Colonel William F. Friedman,
Who Deciphered the Japanese Code
in World War II

Introduction

I N THE SUMMER of 1976 the National Security Agency, the intelligence organization which carries on the activities of America's "Black Chamber" — closed in 1929 by Henry Stimson, then secretary of state, on the grounds that "Gentlemen don't read each other's mail" — made great efforts to see the manuscript of Colonel William Friedman's biography, written during the previous three years following research in both the United States and Europe. The world's greatest cryptologist, renowned for his success in breaking the Japanese "Purple Code," Friedman had become special assistant to the agency's director soon after the agency was set up in 1952, and for some years carried out for it a number of important services. He had, in particular, traveled on three top secret missions to Europe in 1957 and 1958, and it was in these missions that the N.S.A. showed such nervous interest.

Although the agency had provided no documents concerning the life of their distinguished employee, its officials began to express what they called "serious concern" about what might have been said in the biography about these missions. Requests to read the manuscript were made both in Britain and the United States. There was a late-in-the-day offer of horse trading — even though the crucial material was already in the biographer's hands. The reason for worry, it was stated in one of several attempts to see what had been written, was that the book might discuss the supply of cipher machines to NATO; and that this would deprive N.S.A. of the daily information enabling the N.S.A. to read the secret messages of other NATO countries.

The ability to read all NATO messages was no doubt a natural aim in the aftermath of Suez. It had then seemed that while N.S.A. was able to monitor and decipher many of the British and French communications, the agency was not able to decipher them all. Ideally, the situation would be that of the early 1920s when members of the Black Chamber were not only reading the most secret instructions sent to the Japanese delegates to the Washington Disarmament Conference but had access to the messages sent by the British ambassador. In 1957 there was also another slight worry. If many, although not all, of the enciphered British and French messages could be read by the Americans, then the tables might be turned in the future, a possibility that naturally disturbed the officials in N.S.A. headquarters at Fort George G. Meade.

Only one man was capable of resolving the situation to America's advantage: William Friedman, who despite having suffered three severe heart attacks, being in constant danger of sudden death, and more than once under psychiatric treatment, was sent on his delicate missions.

These were, in official eyes, the crowning achievements of Friedman's career, as important to America in the 1960s as his breaking of Purple had been to the country in the Second World War. Friedman's problem was basically that of seeing into the cryptological future, of estimating what measures, overt and covert, would have to be taken by America in the years ahead to counter new machines that might be introduced by Europe's various makers of cipher machines.

This would have been a distasteful and delicate enough mission for any man. It was doubly so for Friedman who over the years had built up a genuine friendship with his British counterparts, and who could now only guess at the course which the special Anglo-U.S. relationship might take in the future.

It is significant that from 1957 onward Friedman's private correspondence shows a growing disillusion not only with the N.S.A. — perhaps an inevitable reaction by a master of cryptography — but with some implications of the profession to which he had devoted his life. N.S.A.'s reclassification on security grounds of documents which had been public for years gave him little confidence in the judgment or maturity of his masters. The confiscation by the agency of nearly fifty items from his own private cryptographic collection was an act of folly which gave him less. But when Friedman appeared to wash his palms, quoting Macbeth — "Will all great Neptune's ocean wash this blood clean from my hand?" — it was not of muddled inefficiency that he was thinking; nor when he muttered of his work, as he sometimes did, "how on earth did I get into this business?"

There is, perhaps, nothing so very remarkable about all this. Since the setting-up of America's Black Chamber after the First World War it has been increasingly true throughout the world that on an international level gentlemen do try to read each other's mail. The British, after all, had been doing it with only minor interruptions since Henry VIII had created the organization which had led, less than fifty years later, to Mary Queen of Scots having her head chopped from her pretty neck. Even so, there are inevitably times when what a manuscript history of the U.S. Signal Corps in Friedman's collection calls the "general use of codes by nations, part of a universal trespass recognized quite apart from conventional standards of international morality," sticks in the gullet of honorable men.

With Friedman the situation was to be compounded: by his desperate loyalty to America, by his shame at some of the things which were done in her name, and by the shadows of his early family background.

Chapter One

Preparation

K ISHINEV IS TODAY the capital of the Moldavian Soviet Socialist Republic, a city of nearly three hundred thousand inhabitants built on the banks of the River Byk, a tributary of the Dneister. At the end of the nineteenth century it was a third the size, a town still recovering from its centuries as shuttlecock between the Russians to the east and the Rumanians to the west, a polyglot center through whose wide acacia-lined streets jostled a shifting population of Moldavians, Wallachs, Russians, Tartars, Germans and Tziganes. Little more than a hundred miles to the south lay the Black Sea port of Odessa; to the north and northwest, rolling country stretched up towards the foothills of the Carpathians and the mountain passes beyond which lay Hungary, Austria, and the baroque empire of Franz Joseph. Part crossroads, part trading center for the tobacco, fruit and wine harvested from an amenable surrounding countryside, Kishinev was a town of seemingly built-in contradictions: a comfortable center of near-prosperity, yet a town with a rambling, ambling air where few families had deep roots.

Here Wolfe — later to become William — Frederic Friedman was born in 1891, the son of Frederic Friedman, a Rumanian Jew from Bucharest. The father, something of a linguist, had moved to Kishinev by the age of twenty and in 1887 became an interpreter and translator in the Russian Postal Service. Within two years he had married Rosa Trust, daughter of a prosperous Kishinev wine merchant. Little is known of either family's background, but filtering up through folk memory are recollections of Rosa traveling through snow-covered streets in a sable-lined drosky, of good food and drink, a picture of the prosperous bourgeois life described by Pushkin, who lived in the town for three years. It is not certain that father and mother came from basically different layers of society; even had they done so, the less class-conscious structure of American life, into which they were soon to become immersed, would have done much to remove any awkward legacies. Nevertheless, William Friedman was to develop a dichotomy of outlook which made him at times a profoundly unhappy man, and it is not too fanciful to see some hint of cause for it in the contrast between minor civil servant and well-to-do merchant's daughter.

The Friedmans' cozy existence was abandoned with good reason a year after the birth of their first son. Many of Kishinev's doctors, lawyers and merchants were Jews. So also, by the 1890s, was more than half the population; indeed, three-quarters of the little local factories were owned by Jews. Despite their comparative prosperity — or possibly because of it — they were soon to bear the full brunt of an anti-Semitic tyranny quite as pointless as that of today's barbarous rule.

Following the assassination of Alexander II in 1881, Russia's

Jews had been increasingly hemmed in and harried by the government restrictions which slowly but steadily spread out from Moscow towards the more distant provinces of the Empire. By 1891 even the great southern capital of Kiev was drastically affected by a new spate of anti-Semitic rules and regulations while from Moscow itself no less than 76,000 Jews pulled up roots in that year alone, and left their native homeland, most of them bound for the United States.

Frederic Friedman foresaw what was to come: the pogrom of a decade later when in Kishinev alone hundreds were killed and injured, seven hundred Jewish homes destroyed and six hundred Jewish businesses wrecked. In the summer of 1892 he sailed for the United States, arrived in Pittsburgh, and had soon established himself as a door-to-door salesman for Singer sewing machines. His wife followed with their son and a daughter in 1893, traveling steerage. Thus at the end of the century the Friedmans were among those

> *. . . who dreamt our basic dream*
> *In that old world while still a serf of kings,*
> *Who dreamt a dream so strong, so brave, so true,*
> *That even yet its mighty daring sings*
> *In every brick and stone, in every furrow turned*
> *That's made America the land it has become.*

Wolfe Friedman, who officially became William when his father, in 1896, "renounced allegiance to the czar of Russia" and became an American citizen, had no vestigial memory of his homeland and no personal experience of the persecution which had driven his young parents west. What he did have was something deeper than the insecurity of the emigrant down the ages, the insecurity which for the Friedmans in America was the result of the constant struggle to make both ends meet; indeed, as the son would recall in later

9

life, the family was always in debt. More important than this financial struggle was the background of news from what his parents had always known as home. "Colonel Friedman," says a psychiatrist who treated him more than half a century later, "was plagued by all sorts of trials and tribulations, many of which came from outside. . . . He remembered from his childhood the great fear of pogroms." This residual memory — not of his own experiences but of the family's latest news — would have been important to any keen intellect; it was doubly so to Friedman, immersed as he was to become for the greater part of his life in a cloak-and-dagger world where no holds were barred. The memory, moreover, hardened up with the years, and eventually William Friedman suspected that, despite outward appearances, official Washington's attitude toward the Jews was different in degree rather than in kind from that of the Russian governors of Moldavia. Although it is difficult to substantiate, Jewish ancestry may well have been a handicap in government employment between the two world wars. Certainly Friedman felt this so strongly that only two months before he died, he wrote to a friend asking: "By the way, will you contribute to the Foundation to the Presidency of which I have just elected myself — a Foundation seeking five billion dollars (U.S.) for the five thousand years of oppression to which thousands of my ancestors and myself were subjected by the enlightened non-Jews of all the countries of all the continents of the world?"

This disillusion lay far ahead as the Friedmans settled down in Pittsburgh to the tough task of building a new life in alien surroundings. While the father worked his way upward in Singer's, the mother became a customer's peddler for a clothing firm, traveling through the city's suburbs and bringing potential customers in to the wholesalers. It was a hard life. It would have been harder still but for the driving force of Rosa Friedman, running with an iron discipline a family that eventually included four sons, a daughter, and a resolutely orthodox Jewish grandfather who left Russia when the Friedmans had established themselves in their new home.

The arrival of the patriarch quickly brought the family back once more into the traditions of the strictly kosher household, which they had almost abandoned on settling in Pittsburgh. Not all its members were happy about the reversion and one of the young Friedman's first memories was of bread being brought to the table with its buttered side facing down. Thus Grandfather would not see that butter and meat were on the table at the same time. The contrast between what was expected and what was done may well have helped create the ambivalent and self-worrying views about religion that developed as the boy grew up. Recording his faith as Jewish on a score of official forms, he wore the faith lightly, with an air that concealed a continual questioning: was it right to do one thing and profess another? The question would have been a nagging one for any man of intelligence; it was to be doubly so in a professional field where success was often equated with deception.

From the first it was clear that William Friedman was different from the rest of the family, and in a conformist society he showed an angularity which kept him somewhat apart even from his brothers. When told to rewrite a competition speech praising a local Socialist leader then in prison, or rule himself out of the contest, he refused to rewrite a word. But he still won the competition. As he grew up he would play chess with his brothers on the steps of their home; he would describe grandiose plans for reviving the world's agriculture; and at times he would talk with a trace of excitement about a world he had discovered through Edgar Allan Poe's "The Gold Bug."

It is not known where Friedman came upon the story, which had been extensively printed and reprinted in magazines and journals. Yet there is no doubt that its chance discovery prepared him for the work ahead, and little doubt that without it he would not have slipped so easily from his first-chosen profession into the work that was to affect the course of the Second World War. Although Poe is best known for his stories of terror and the grotesque, he was also an amateur cryptographer. He wrote more than one article on the subject, offered to decipher any secret messages for the journal that published them, and once agreed to solve encipherments that had as their key any phrase in French, Italian, Spanish, German, Latin or Greek. In "The Gold Bug," moreover, Poe used an enciphered message as clue to the discovery of an immense hoard of buried treasure. It was a subject to arouse enthusiasm and Friedman, hooked on buried treasure, became hooked on the means of finding it. Half a lifetime later he was still prepared to waste time on the most unlikely of "buried treasure" messages sent to him for decipherment.

As a boy, Friedman epitomized the ambitious Jewish immigrant's son, determined to get to the top of the ladder and concentrating everything on that one aim. In 1909, when he graduated from Pittsburgh Central High School, a main interest was electrical engineering, and with the birth of electromechanical enciphering little more than a decade away, this might eventually have brought him directly into the cryptographic stream. He was, however, to reach it by a more circuitous route.

In the high school there existed a debating society, the "Emporean Philomath," and at its weekly meetings the members became imbued with the idea of a Jewish "back to the soil" movement, an idea that brought with it the ambition of becoming pioneering scientific agriculturalists. Friedman was one of five who were sufficiently enthusiastic to persuade their parents they should join the Michigan Agricultural College at Lansing. He worked to earn his expenses, and matriculated into the college in the autumn of 1909, left after six months, and in 1911 was accepted by Cornell University as an undergraduate, by this time attracted to the new science of genetics now growing up from the rediscovery of Mendel's work in 1900. Thus it was as a geneticist, anxious to make two ears of corn grow where one had grown before, that Friedman first determined to make his mark in the world.

Fieldwork formed part of his undergraduate studies, and in the summer of 1913 he was helping Dr. G.H. Shull at the Carnegie Institution's Department of Experimental Evolution at Cold Spring Harbor, Long Island. Shull later became renowned for his work in developing hybrid corn but in 1913 his main interest was the chemical basis and heredity of sex mutations and aberrations, and various problems of heredity.

Friedman was now twenty-two, dark haired, trim, dapper, and strikingly good looking, a junior version of the Adolphe Menjou figure he was to become. And at Cold Spring Harbor he met Verna Lehman, a young Brooklyn girl. "We — my folks, my little brother and my little boy cousin — were staying there for the summer, and I met him when he was working in a field of flowers, crossing them like Burbank did," she remembered in the 1970s. "I guess I fell in love with him the minute I met him, and he came to see me every evening until he went back to college and we went home. I considered Will the finest young man I ever knew and I would have married him if he had asked me."

Years later he explained why he did not. "You were (and, I imagine, still are)" he wrote, "so beautiful I think I completely lost my heart and it scared me because I was then so unprepared to contemplate a more serious relationship, for I was still in College. I knew I *had* to complete the course and hence my head told me: 'Do that first, and then we'll see.' "

The if's of history are rarely worth much consideration. But if Friedman had married Verna Lehman, he might never have been diverted into cryptography; he would certainly not have married the woman who became the distaff half of the world's most famous cryptographic husband-and-wife team; and the Japanese Purple code would not have been broken as it was, with all that that was to mean for the course of the Second World War.

William Friedman working in the Cold Spring Harbor, Long Island, grounds of the Carnegie Institution's Department of Experimental Evolution in the summer of 1913.

William Friedman and Verna Lehman, Brooklyn, 1913.

William Friedman prior to his graduation from Cornell University.

In 1914 Friedman graduated from Cornell with a B.S. and prepared to launch himself on a career in genetics. The first move was enrollment as a graduate student in the university's College of Agriculture. For the following eighteen months he spent two-thirds of his time studying plant breeding, plant physiology, botany and chemistry in the university's Department of Plant Breeding; during the other third he taught undergraduates. He had registered for the course leading to a Ph.D. but after six months unaccountably switched to an M.S.A. course, a move that later led to the comment that his record had "been somewhat irregular."

Nevertheless the prospect that stretched ahead was still that of a purely academic life. It was soon to be drastically changed.

In May, 1915, Friedman's supervisor, Professor Rollins A. Emerson, received a letter out of the blue from a Colonel George Fabyan of Chicago. The colonel wrote on the letter-head paper of Bliss, Fabyan & Co., a prosperous firm of cotton merchants, and explained that he needed a properly qualified man to take charge of the Department of Genetics he was starting at his Riverbank Laboratories, a three-hundred-acre estate at Geneva, some thirty miles from Chicago. Did the professor know some bright young man who would be suitable?

Whether Emerson knew anything at all about Fabyan is not certain, but seems unlikely. Had he done so he might have been less willing to help. However, the professor made enquiries among his graduates, found Friedman agreeable, and proposed that he write to Chicago.

The young man's state of mind at the time, and his willingness to throw overboard the prospect of an academic future, are revealed in a letter to a friend. "I had notions of scratching a living out of the soil when the 'back to the farm' movement hit this country in 1910" he admitted. "A few weeks of preparation for the 'return' showed me that Mother Nature got the wrong number when I answered that call. But I was impecunious and could not afford to pay for the kind of training that I really was cut out for, electrical engineering, so I specialised in what seemed to offer great possibilities for research and ingenuity, genetics. After graduation and almost two years of work in the graduate school, it seemed advisable to start in to see how hard making a living really is, so I quit and went to Chicago where a certain rich man set me up with a laboratory on his estate, paid me to experiment, and generally had a good time and lots of publicity to the chagrin of the few 'curiosities' like myself who lived on the place."

There was a brief meeting between "rich man" Fabyan and Friedman early in June and on the fourteenth Fabyan wrote to his prospective employee a letter which gave the young Friedman a shrewd idea of the man he was dealing with. The colonel offered a hundred dollars a month and explained that his geneticist, like the rest of his staff, would live on the Riverbank Estate. The appointment would thus include board and lodging; but there would be no contract. "I might not like you and you might not like the job, and there is no use making a fool contract, any more than there is in signing a lease for a house, which is usually a waste of time provided either side wants to break it," the writer explained.

I am not looking for a man to duplicate work that is being done at every agricultural station in the country, and at every advanced school and university. I am not capable of bossing your work or you, but I am capable of recognising hard, earnest, sincere endeavour, whether it results in success or not. We talked enough about this to make any further comments on this point superfluous. If you start in, I will give you some rope, and see how you handle yourself. I should be interested and deem it necessary for you to continue your studies, with the objective point of

getting the advanced degree. I certainly don't want you to
remain at Riverbank until you get so darned narrow that
you would be useless. I would expect you to affiliate yourself with some university, to be decided upon, and occasionally visit them or others. If I should hear of something
anywhere this side of Hell that I thought would do us any
good, I might want you to go there and find out about it;
in other words, I don't want you to go backwards. . . .

Friedman liked Fabyan's bluff outspokenness just as he was later
attracted by at least some of the man's grandiose schemes, by the
attitude of one who, when asked about the value of genetics could
reply: "Why, look at the average human being. A mighty pitiful
contraption of flesh and bones. If we of the Riverbank community
can improve the human race by experimenting first with flowers
and plants, won't that be a wonderful thing?" The attraction was
strong enough to counteract the less agreeable features of the lord
of the Riverbank Estate, the colonel who had never served in the
army, since his rank was an honorary one awarded by the governor
of Illinois.

There were further meetings and Friedman eventually agreed to
take up the post in September, after he had completed his teaching
at Cornell. Before this, he received one more letter which underlined the attitude of the man who was, by a quirk of chance, to set
him on the road to becoming the greatest cryptologist the world
had known.

"Here is a problem that has come up in my mind, that I want
you to work on," he was told by Fabyan.

I want the father of wheat, and I want a wife for him, so
that the child will grow in arid country. Where did I get
this problem? I got it from one of my wealthy Jewish
friends, and if I can beat him to it, he will foot the bills
and be damned glad to. To gain my point I would rip every

Colonel George Fabyan in his "Hell Chair" at Riverbank.

Japanese Garden of the Fabyan estate at Geneva, Illinois, 1917. Left to right on the island are William Friedman's mother, his youngest brother and Elizebeth Friedman

The Fabyan estate showing giant web. Woven of heavy rope, it measured sixty feet in diameter and served as a backdrop to the outdoor "sitting space" where guests assembled for lively conversation.

rose out of every greenhouse at Riverbank, if it seemed to be part of wisdom to do so, even though I had the certain knowledge that failure was staring me in the face. Failure is going to come, and a lot of them, and a lot of disappointment, loss after loss, but as long as it is done intelligently, and we know why, I have no kick coming.

Now this is enough for you to chew on. Riverbank is not going to be a one-man outfit. Those that are there today, including yourself, are going to pass on candidates for the different positions as they come up. As soon as we are able to do some instructing, arrangements will be made along those lines. We will not seek outside donations.

This may seem impractical and improbable, but I have seen impracticable and improbable things accomplished, provided the direction was practical, and based on sound business principles. I could go on indefinitely, but what is the use? We play the game from day to day the best we can.

The colonel's search for tougher strains of wheat involved some odd methods, not least being the sowing of seed at various phases of the moon. However, such bizarre practices were almost commonplace in the curious world of the Riverbank Estate where Friedman found himself in the autumn of 1915.

George Fabyan came from a distinguished Boston family. His father had been head of the Bliss Fabyan Corporation, then the largest cotton goods organization in the world, and it had been anticipated that the son would step into the father's shoes. So he did, but only after running away from home as a boy, being disinherited, then returning to the fold after joining the family firm under another name and creating such a remarkable sales record that the head of the firm insisted on meeting the unknown young man. Father met son, all was forgiven, and on Father's death a few years later, George Fabyan inherited not only three million dollars but control of the firm's Chicago office. This he ran with a good deal of mordant humor. A visitor, for instance, might pick up an elaborately bound brochure entitled: "What I Know About the Future of Cotton and Domestic Goods: by George Fabyan." Inside, there were a hundred blank pages.

The successful running of Fabyan's Chicago office was a sideline when compared with the complexities of Riverbank, where he developed his hobbies. "Some rich men go in for art collections, gay times on the Riviera, or extravagant living," he once said. "But they all get satiated. That's why I stick to scientific experiments, spending money to discover valuable things that universities can't afford. You never get sick of too much knowledge."

The knowledge was sought in an unusual setting. Guests were sometimes met at the local railway station by limousine and chauffeur, sometimes by Fabyan himself, the coachman of a carriage drawn by zebras. The grounds into which visitors were taken incorporated a bear pit for vegetarian bears, a Japanese garden planned by one of the emperor's gardeners and a Roman bathing pool. There was also a German windmill bought shortly before Friedman arrived on the estate. Its function was indicated in a brief note from Fabyan, which said: "Have just got old German windmill with old fashioned stones to grind wheat to flour and other grist. Can you pick up competent man who understands the old German grist mill?"

Inside the Villa, where Fabyan lived with his wife, and through which his pet gorilla roamed at will, the first features noticed by visitors were the divans, chairs — and even beds — which throughout the house did not sit on legs but swung from the beams on huge chains. The master matched the surroundings, a thickset man, bearded and bellowing, whose youthful escapades had precluded formal education but who had picked up the trick of parroting any technical information he might hear, a characteristic which took in all but the most cautious. On the estate he dressed in a curious knickerbocker suit that parodied the riding habit of an earlier age — although he himself had never ridden a horse and had no intention of doing so. Ordering the lives of his staff with authoritarian disdain for their wishes or their self-respect, Fabyan was the most unlikely man to win loyalty; that he won it from William Friedman, and that it survived a long series of double-dealings that would have shocked most men, suggests some under-lying quality which he normally concealed. Perhaps it was his own form of honesty. Asked what he did on his estate, he replied: "I raise Hell."

In fact, as Friedman was soon to discover, Fabyan did a good deal more. In his cotton business he had, like most other business-men, employed simple codes and ciphers to conceal salient facts in telegrams and cables. He therefore had a point of contact with Mrs. Elizabeth Wells Gallup to whom he was introduced by rich Boston friends. Mrs. Gallup was attempting to prove, as others had at-tempted before her, that Francis Bacon was the real author of Shakespeare's works. She was, moreover, trying to do so by discov-ering, in the First Folios of Shakespeare, the enciphered messages that she believed had been put there by Bacon.

Fabyan, attracted by the idea itself as well as by its publicity potential, brought Mrs. Gallup under his wing, setting her up on the Riverbank Estate with all the secretarial and other help she required. Then, just as an interest in ciphers for business purposes had led him on to Mrs. Gallup and the alleged Baconian cipher, so did Bacon lead him on to another activity. Among the prolifera-tion of Baconian ideas was one for a levitating device; this consisted of a circular cylinder with wires stretched outside it from end to end. If these were tuned to a major chord, it was claimed, and then vibrated as the cylinder rotated, the whole contraption would rise into the air of its own accord. Fabyan had the idea of building such a device, and a brother at Harvard conveniently put him in touch with Professor Wallace Sabine, a university physicist and America's leading expert on architectural acoustics. Nothing seems to have come of the levitating device but Sabine was invited to build his own acoustics laboratory at Riverbank, and preparations were under way when Friedman arrived.

However, anti-Stratfordianism and acoustics were not the only activities on which the colonel was prepared to expend time, thought and money. There was, almost inevitably, research on a perpetual motion device. A Dr. Scott, one of the most prominent physicians and surgeons in the country, carried out such medical investigations as interested Fabyan, especially those connected with the use of the radioactive materials discovered a decade and more earlier by the Curies. A prominent veterinary surgeon was trying at Riverbank to discover a cure for the hoof and mouth disease, which had been decimating the livestock of the Middle West. And to this heterogeneous collection there was now added the Department of Genetics.

Few details have survived of Friedman's work as a geneticist. It is known that he was testing the Mendelian laws of heredity with fruit flies and plants, and a letter written in September to Dr. Beverly T. Galloway at Cornell throws a faint gleam of light on his activities. "Knowing that you have written on the subject of violets," he said, "I am hoping to secure some information on the subject from you. Can you tell me where I can secure a collection of varieties and species of the horticultural violet? In my cereal greenhouse I have one bench in which I should like to grow as many types as possible with a view to improvement later. What do you think of the possibilities of improving this flower?"

Dr. Galloway was hardly encouraging. "So far as I am aware," he replied, "no one has undertaken any work on the improvement of the violet. It is a difficult crop to handle. The double varieties are subject to serious diseases and are going out of use. The single varieties are becoming much more extensively grown and used, but they all have characteristics which are more or less objectionable," he concluded.

From the standpoint of contemporary genetics, it sounds simple enough. But Mendelism had been recognized for what it was only fifteen years earlier, and the first years of the twentieth century were largely occupied in confirming the basic principles of how heredity worked. There was much darkness, little light, and not until the year that Friedman went to Riverbank were Morgan, Sturtevant, Muller and Bridges able to interpret Mendel's results in terms of the chromosome theory. The dominance of the mathematician in genetics had barely begun, and it would have been surprising if Friedman had done more than confirm existing theories during the short while he was working full-time on the subject for Colonel Fabyan. And within a few months of arriving at Riverbank he had been drawn into the field of cryptography; within less than a year it was his main occupation and the work of the genetics department, of which he remained formally the director, was being carried out by a young woman assistant.

Chapter Two

Initiation

FRIEDMAN'S INDUCTION into what became his life's work was directly due to the activities of Mrs. Elizabeth Wells Gallup. An American woman in her middle sixties, she had been educated in Paris and Marburg. She had taught English in Michigan for some twenty years and become the principal of a high school. She had also, long before being brought to the Riverbank Laboratories by Colonel Fabyan, become firmly convinced not only that Sir Francis Bacon was the real author of Shakespeare but that this could be shown by deciphering messages she believed were incorporated in the texts of the plays. Baconian authorship had first been suggested as long ago as 1785 and other candidates had been added from time to time: Roger Manners, the 5th Earl of Rutland; William Stanley, the 6th Earl of Derby; Edward de Vere, the 17th Earl

Mrs. Elizabeth Wells Gallup (front row, far left) at Riverbank, c. 1916, with a group of her helpers. Elizebeth Smith, later Mrs. William Friedman, is standing behind central figure in front row. The tall man at center rear is Dr. J. A. Powell, later Captain Powell, liaison officer between Riverbank Laboratories and Army Headquarters in France.

of Oxford. Even Anne Hathaway, Shakespeare's wife, even Queen Elizabeth herself, were put forward as possibilities. The claim for Bacon appeared less unsupportable than the others, since, if cipher messages could establish authorship, a cipher was ready to hand. This was Bacon's own biliteral cipher, briefly touched upon in his *The Advancement of Learning* and later described more fully in his *De Augmentis Scientiarum.*

The cipher, to the disinterment of which in the Shakespeare plays Mrs. Gallup devoted much of her adult life, involved the use of two letters in such a way that they could represent any letter in the alphabet. The letter A would thus be represented by aaaaa, the letter B by aaaab, the letter C by aaaba, the letter D by aaabb, and so on through the alphabet. The message GOOD NEWS would in this cipher be represented by the letters:

aabba abbab abbab aaabb abbaa aabaa babaa baaab

To send this it is first necessary to make up a sentence having five times as many letters as those in the original message, or in other words, a message having as many letters as the combined "a"s and "b"s in the encipherment — for instance, WE WILL SEE YOU ON SUNDAY OR SOME OTHER PROPER DAY; then to fit the cipher to the message and underline each letter that is below a "b." Thus:

a abbaabbabbabbab aaabbab
We w i l l s e e y o u o n S u n d a y o r

baa aabaababaabaaab
s o m e o t h e r p r o p e r d a y

The longer message — WE WILL SEE YOU ON SUNDAY OR SOME OTHER PROPER DAY — is then sent, with the unmarked letters being written in the ordinary way and the marked letters written in italic. The recipient merely has to perform the operations in reverse by writing an "a" under the letters written in the ordinary way and writing a "b" under the rest. Reference to the alphabet showing A as aaaaa and B as aaaab then provides the enciphered message of GOOD NEWS.

The one essential of the biliteral cipher is that the letters involved shall be written in one of two different ways, such as italic and roman. Now Mrs. Gallup, who had first been drawn to the Baconian theory by Orville Ward Owen, a Detroit physician, had worked on the facsimile editions of the First Folios available in the United States. She was struck by the apparently arbitrary use of italic type, roman type and a third form, which the printer calls swash italic letters, and by the fact that there did appear to be differences in letter-shape in all three types, as though the printer had used different kinds of type, or fonts as they are called. Here, Mrs. Gallup believed, was Bacon's biliteral cipher in use. Here, if she could only decide which letters were of the "a" form and which of the "b," would be found the hidden messages proving Baconian authorship.

Although any reason for concealing the authorship is still somewhat obscure, there was sufficient incentive to press on, and in 1899 she had produced *The Biliteral Cypher of Sir Francis Bacon Discovered in His Works and Deciphered by Mrs. Elizabeth Wells Gallup.* The book stirred up both criticism and commendation. What it failed to do was arouse any significant scholarly acclaim. Mrs. Gallup followed up with much study in Oxford and another two books. Then, on her return to the United States, she was introduced to Colonel Fabyan by Mrs. Kate Prescott of Boston, an indefatigable lady whom Friedman was later to describe as "a kind of contact-woman of the Baconian underworld or, to vary the metaphor, the liaison agent between the American cells of international anti-Stratfordianism."

Colonel Fabyan's support of Mrs. Gallup was not entirely disinterested. As Friedman and his wife were later to say: "It was not far from his mind that if Bacon were proved to be Shakespeare, Mrs. Gallup would also be seen to be (administratively and financially) Colonel Fabyan, which would be very satisfactory." As a result he provided her, and her sister Kate Wells, with quarters and staff. All the Riverbank resources were to be hers on demand, and it was this state of affairs which, early in 1916, gave Friedman his first serious contact with cryptography.

From the start, Mrs. Gallup had always agreed that the differences between the "a" letters and the "b" letters in the Baconian cipher were small. Later researches showed beyond all doubt that such differences as existed were due to worn type, damaged type, imperfections in the paper, or what the printer knows as ink-spread. Heresies of this kind were always ruled out of court by both Fabyan and Mrs. Gallup who believed that the differences, visible only with difficulty to the naked eye, would be seen more clearly in photographic enlargement. It was there that Friedman was brought into the story. A self-taught but skilled photographer, he now found his services conscripted into Mrs. Gallup's Baconian operation. For some weeks he devoted a good deal of his time to photographing individual letters in a variety of Elizabethan books, producing greatly enlarged prints, and then listening to Mrs. Gallup's exposition of their alleged differences as she assigned them to the "a" class or the "b" class.

There was more to it than photography, however. Fabyan had brought to Riverbank a number of students who were instructed in the work of deciphering by Mrs. Gallup. Some came from well-known colleges and universities, some from high schools and some, as Friedman later commented, "were without much formal education, the peculiar nature of the work in cryptography requiring peculiarly constituted minds." All were trained at Fabyan's expense and, once having gained the necessary proficiency, were given a salary and set to work by Mrs. Gallup.

Inevitably, Friedman's enquiring mind began working on the cryptographic problems as well as the photographic: first, on the genuine as distinct from the imaginary differences between the "a" forms and the "b" forms of the letters; later, on the underlying principles by which the biliteral cipher, or any other, could be used to incorporate hidden messages in an apparently innocuous text. More remarkably, Friedman now found that he himself possessed one of those "peculiarly constituted minds" which is the first essential of the born cryptologist. But he had another advantage since, as a friend later wrote: "He started young enough not to be scared of the magnitude of the problems facing him: had he been a Ph.D. with three or four years' postgraduate training he could have been ruined."

Mrs. Gallup was concerned with cryptography for a single specific purpose; thus she was more interested in ends than means. With Friedman the reverse was to be the case; it was the demand for skill which attracted him rather than the purposes for which it was used, and it is significant that his first contact with the subject involved a literary detective operation without hint of the moral ambiguities which riddle the use of cryptography for intelligence purposes. In later life he would sometimes quote Macbeth, pretend to wash his hands, and make it clear that he wanted to clean the blood from them. Had he sensed the future he might have stuck to genetics.

Even so, once his intellect had been seized of the subject, it would have been difficult for him to abandon it for something different. One reason was that his mind was ideally tuned to deal with the special problems of cryptography.

Throughout a life devoted exclusively to the subject Friedman often tried to analyze that quality which enabled one man to pull a cryptographic solution from the hat when other men, apparently better qualified, certainly as mentally nimble, continued to flounder in despair. Some mathematical facility helped, and very early in his career Friedman was to construct a fresh and mathematically based foundation on which the principles of cryptography could be erected; more than any other man he changed the craft from one run predominantly by guess and by God to one in which certain scientific principles had to be rigorously followed. Yet just as Einstein always stressed the need for intuition in scientific discovery, so did Friedman believe that the same thing, however named, was useful to the cryptologist and essential to the cryptanalyst whose task it is to break codes and cipher. Describing a colleague's solution of one particularly difficult problem, he was reluctant "to call it 'guesswork' if the impression is left that such a solution is unworthy of the cryptanalyst." On an article entitled "Let your subconscious solve it," he noted how important it was to remember that admonition "when one raises the question as to how sometimes suddenly the cryptanalyst gets an idea which enables him to proceed and pass the mental road block that has hampered his progress." And on a paper discussing insight he wrote in his rounded careful hand: "A cryptologist without creative insight is only half a cryptologist."

As Friedman once summed up, with the exception of a few simple ciphers and codes, "nearly every scientifically constructed cryptographic system presents a unique case in cryptanalysis, the unravelling of which requires the exercise of unusual powers of observation, inductive and deductive reasoning, much concentration, perseverance and a vivid imagination; but all these qualities are of little avail without a special aptitude arising from extensive practical experience." Thus the cryptographer who devises fresh ways of enciphering and thereby concealing messages, and the cryptanalyst who discovers methods of decipherment, both need, as well as other qualities, not only imagination but also an indefinable flair for the subject.

The expertise is needed equally when dealing with either codes or ciphers. While both serve the same purpose of concealing the plaintext of a message — what the sender is saying to the receiver — they do so in rather different ways. In a code system both sender and receiver have identical code-books: lists of words, phrases, sentences or numbers, each of which can be used in an encoded message to represent a letter, syllable or word of plaintext. Encoding demands the substitution of the various elements in the plaintext with their equivalents in the code-book, and these encoded equivalents are later turned back into the elements of the plaintext by the receiver who merely has to look at his own code-book to discover what these are.

In such a code, the individual elements encoded can be of different lengths; for instance the word "advance" can be encoded by the word "picket" or the number 1002, and the word "dawn" can be encoded by the word "enemy" or the number 2131. With ciphers, however, the units to be enciphered are of the same length; they may be single letters, pairs of letters, or sometimes sets of three letters, but in each case they are taken as symbols rather than as component parts of words or sentences. The letters are enciphered by the use of two things: a set of unvarying rules known as the general system; and a specific, but variable, key which may be a word or a number governing the various steps to be taken under the general system. The cipher systems that result are usually of one of two kinds: transposition systems, which, as their name suggests, involve the rearrangement of the letters in the message to be sent; and substitution systems, which require the replacement of the letters in the plaintext by other letters or symbols. Both methods can be combined in a single system to make decipherment more difficult.

In very general terms, the more complex a cipher system, then the smaller the chance of its being deciphered without the key. However, complex systems demand more time and ability than simple ones, both for encipherment and decipherment. They are also more vulnerable to mistakes. In military use, therefore, a

Elizebeth Smith and Colonel George Fabyan at the Riverbank Laboratories, Geneva, Illinois, summer 1916.

William Friedman at Riverbank, 1916.

William and Elizebeth Friedman soon after they were married at Riverbank, 1917.

cipher system that its users think can be broken by not less than two days' work might justifiably be employed for messages whose significance would have disappeared after two hours.

A man who devotes his life to making or breaking such systems needs a special incentive. It is unlikely to come from the prospect of riches, since cryptographers who make codes and ciphers and cryptanalysts who break them are not unduly well rewarded. It cannot come from fame in the usual sense of the word, and Friedman often underlined that "a necessary (though far from sufficient) requirement for happiness, as a cryptanalyst, is a passion for anonymity." His own incentive was compounded of two factors. One was enjoyment in deploying what he knew were his unique abilities — "after all is said and done, if you like your work, there isn't much else that matters," he once wrote. The other he revealed when asked what had initially made him take up cryptography: "Just an inherent curiosity to know what people were trying to write that they didn't want other people to read," he replied.

The anti-Stratfordians who could not bring themselves to believe that Shakespeare wrote Shakespeare were often used by Friedman to illustrate what he saw as operations on the lunatic fringe of cryptography, a definition from which he excluded those of Mrs. Gallup. Sane and honest, but misled and gullible, was his early verdict on her, reinforced as his purely photographic part in her work gave way to study of the theory and practice of what she was doing.

His interest in the alleged subtle differences between the "a" letters in a photographic copy of a First Folio passage and the neighboring "b" letters was soon complemented by an interest in one of Mrs. Gallup's helpers. She was Elizebeth Smith — Elizebeth with an "e" since her mother hoped the spelling would prevent her being called "Eliza" — whose ancestors had arrived in the United States with William Penn in 1682. Nearly a century later the family traveled west to Virginia where her grandfather was later read out of the Quakers for taking part in the War of 1812. Shortly afterwards the family moved again, some members settling in Ohio where Elizebeth's father was born before the family went on once more, this time to Huntington, Indiana, then only an Indian trading post. Here Elizebeth Smith was born in the last years of the nineteenth century, the youngest of nine children. As a graduate in English literature she almost casually visited Chicago's Newberry Reference Library in 1916 to study the library's First Folio. An enquiry about jobs brought an introduction to Colonel Fabyan and by early summer Miss Smith was installed at Riverbank.

She still remembers her first meeting with the man who was to become her husband. "I was on the porch of the Lodge, the house where we all dined with Mrs. Gallup, and he came up the steps. He was a kind of Beau Brummel; no country informality but impeccably dressed as though he had been going to a well-to-do city home."

William Friedman and Elizebeth Smith were two of the relatively few young people at Riverbank. They toured the surrounding countryside together on bicycles. They discussed the day-to-day work on the biliteral cipher and as their friendship grew each recognized in the other that essential "peculiarity of mind." The first outcome of that recognition was a frank exchange of views about Mrs. Gallup's Baconian operation. Each reinforced the other's doubts about the casual way in which "a" letters and "b" letters were identified, invariably to help decipherment of the passage in hand. Putting a finger on the scales, even though subconsciously, seemed a polite euphemism for what they felt was going on.

Friedman was now twenty-five, with a future in genetics stretching out somewhat unsteadily before him amid growing warnings that the United States would soon, inevitably, be drawn into the European war. Miss Smith was just twenty-three. If they were similar in having youth and lack of prospects, their backgrounds were uncompromisingly different: on the one hand that of a Jewish family from the eastern extremity of Europe — almost from the ends of the earth it must have seemed; on the other, a background of impeccable Gentile and Anglo-Saxon purity. In only one thing did their ancestry seem to be united: both families had originally sought the United States to avoid persecution.

Nevertheless, it was with some dire family warnings still ringing in the bridegroom's ears that Friedman and Elizebeth Smith were married in Chicago on May 21, 1917, roughly a month after America had declared war on Germany. It was, according to his brother Max, one of the first mixed marriages by anyone from the Jewish quarter of Pittsburgh. "You would have thought that Bill had committed murder," he has said. "If he had still been living in Pittsburgh he would have been ostracised."

39

Chapter Three

From Art to Craft

SOME MONTHS BEFORE Friedman married, he and Elizebeth had been diverted from their work for Mrs. Gallup to something considerably more important. This was the decipherment, for a number of U.S. Government departments, of messages which the departments were themselves unable to handle. Since freelance and unofficial cryptographers were thus handling official government material, it was a curious state of affairs. It was made more so by the fact that many of the messages were from Mexico, a country whose diplomatic relationship with the United States was in bad repair, and that these messages were obtained, as Friedman has said, "by various and entirely surreptitious means from telegraphs and cable offices in Washington and elsewhere in the U.S."

The explanation lay partly in America's cryptographic vulnerability, partly in Fabyan's ambition. Even when the United States entered the war in 1917 the government was unable to call on any cryptographers outside the armed forces and on only the smallest handful inside them. Fabyan, however, had since the start of his interest in the Baconian cipher begun to collect the very fragmentary information on codes and ciphers then available in the United States. This fact, together with efficient wire-pulling in Washington, had led to the flow of messages sent down to Geneva. These were deciphered by Friedman and one or more of Mrs. Gallup's staff, usually without too much trouble, and then sent back to Washington with Colonel Fabyan's compliments. The government therefore had good reason to be grateful to Fabyan, whatever his eccentricities and however arbitrary the manner in which he treated his staff.

By the first months of 1917 it was clear to many Americans that the United States would, sooner or later and probably sooner, be drawn into the European war. Fabyan was one of them and he now decided to regularize the unofficial situation which had been growing up since the first weeks of the year. On March 17, 1917, he wrote to the Intelligence Office, War Department, in Washington, referring to the work he was already doing for a number of civilian departments and to his own personal expertise as a cryptographer; an expertise, such as it was, which consisted almost entirely of what had rubbed off onto him from his staff. "I was wondering," he went on, "if the information which I had in reference to these ciphers would be of any use to the Government, and if it were possible that the Germans were using any of these old ciphers in transmitting messages in ordinary letters of entirely personal nature. . . ." Almost by return there came a revealing reply from the major-general in charge of military intelligence. "Just at present," he said, "owing to the very limited personnel in the Intelligence Section of the

General Staff, we are not able to take up the study and work on mechanical ciphers." But, he added, another officer would shortly be getting in touch with Riverbank to see what help Fabyan's people could provide.

The decision to grasp Fabyan's proffered straw was a wise move in view of America's extraordinary state of cryptographic unreadiness. Early in 1917 neither the army nor the navy had any organization for intercepting enemy communications, let alone for studying or deciphering them. Only three men in the United States forces had any knowledge of ciphers or of what was involved in their solution: Captain J.O. Mauborgne, later to become head of the U.S. Signal Corps; Captain Parker Hitt, whose *Manual for the Solution of Military Ciphers* included the only readily available material on the subject; and Major Frank Moorman. More remarkably, the new War Department Telegraph Code, introduced in 1915, had been printed in Cleveland by a commercial printer and had no security classification at all; its use, even when apparently made more secure by superencipherment tables, was so unsafe that when the United States entered the war, the British informed Washington that messages sent in it could easily be read. The only other devices available were an old U.S. Cipher Disk and the somewhat comparable British Playfair cipher, both of which could be broken with scarcely greater trouble.

Yet since the outbreak of war in August 1914 between the Central Powers led by Germany and the Allies led by Britain and France, there had been an enormous increase in cryptography and in its counterpart, cryptanalysis. It was not only the exigencies of the war itself which brought about the cryptographic explosion; the use of wireless had suddenly become almost commonplace, not only for sending messages between military units at or near the battle front but between governments hundreds of miles apart. Since interception of wireless messages was comparatively easy and could not be prevented, this development demanded a huge extension of encipherment. In addition, the very volume of messages being sent — and quite possibly intercepted — would require a constant changing of whatever ciphers were being used, as the chances of breaking any enciphered message are clearly linked with the number of messages in the same cipher that can be studied.

The Americans well knew that their slender cryptographic resources would be totally inadequate for dealing with the increase of work in the diplomatic sphere, let alone with the work required to service an army in the field. They therefore turned with relief to Riverbank. There might be some difficulty in putting matters on an official basis, but that would have to wait.

Colonel Mauborgne visited Fabyan in April and on the eleventh, five days after the United States had declared war on Germany, reported that officers should be sent to Riverbank for training, and that the team already working there under Friedman should be used for official deciphering. "The intelligence division of the General Staff, like the Department of Justice, is urged to take immediate advantage of Colonel Fabyan's offer to decipher captured messages," it was reported. "There can be no doubt as to the safety of communications of confidential nature put into his hands, and his laboratories are provided with vaults and other means of protection against fire, theft, and other means of destruction, and his grounds are patrolled against intruders." The Riverbank laboratories in general, and Friedman's cipher department in particular, thus became the theoretically unofficial, but in practice official, cryptographic service of the U.S. Government.

The messages usually arrived by mail, but on occasion urgent problems would be telegraphed to Riverbank, tackled at top speed, and the solutions wired back. Since much of the material still consisted of messages between Germany and Mexico, Spanish and German translators were hired by Fabyan to speed up the work

William Friedman with the A.T. & T. Printing Telegraph Cipher Machine and double key tape.

which was soon coming not only from the army and navy but from the State Department, the Department of Justice and the Censorship and Post Office departments.

This lasted only a few weeks. On June 10 the Cipher Bureau — Military Intelligence 8 — was set up in Washington under the direction of Herbert Yardley, a cipher clerk in the State Department who had been handling the rudimentary methods then employed to protect diplomatic messages. A man of ambition, Yardley was soon occupying a key position in the cryptographic establishment of which the Riverbank group for a while operated as an out-station. The bureau, whose setting-up was a complete break with American tradition, immediately began the interception and attempted decoding of all messages which might help a nation at war. Any potentially effective means were used and the bureau became the first of a long line of organizations which were to operate in much the same way — the American "Black Chamber," the Signal Intelligence Service, the Army Security Agency, and the National Security Agency.

In this field the Americans were inexperienced compared with the British. For three centuries, from 1540 until 1844, The Secret Office, The Private Office and The Deciphering Branch, three linked organizations created by the government, had opened letters, deciphered their contents if necessary, then resealed them and sent them on to their destinations while passing to the Foreign Office any of the contents that might be of interest. Less than fifty years after the organization had been set up by Henry VII it brought spectacular results with the opening of letters from Mary, Queen of Scots, to Antony Babington. They were deciphered by Sir Francis Walsingham, head of Queen Elizabeth's spy service, and found to discuss Queen Elizabeth's assassination. Shortly afterwards the Scots queen was beheaded.

Early in the eighteenth century, operation of the British interception service was for a while theoretically limited; but the war-

45

rants necessary for opening mail were easily obtained and the evidence intercepted and deciphered was frequently accepted in trials, that of Bishop Atterbury, who in 1723 was convicted of plotting a restoration of the Stuarts, being a notable example. The practice continued, although on a smaller scale, until 1844 when the government of the day intercepted the letters of the Italian patriot Giuseppe Mazzini and passed a copy of the contents to the Austrian minister. News of the interception leaked out and in the ensuing scandal — Mazzini having won the enthusiastic support of the British public — the three interception and decipherment offices were closed. But the government's right to open and decipher, although rarely exercised, appears to have remained. Then, in August, 1914, an organization comparable to the three closed offices was started within the Admiralty under wartime regulations. It became famous as Room 40 O.B. and played a vital part in winning the First World War. Its functions were later transferred to the Foreign Office, and it has continued to live on under a succession of titles.

While the Americans were launching their official cryptographic services, the Riverbank staff were given the task of training recruits. A class of four men who had enlisted in the Intelligence Corps and been sent from Washington, was followed by no less than eighty, all of whom had to be given a crash course before being sent overseas. Friedman directed the course, helped by three or four assistants, including Elizebeth Friedman. He lectured daily, supervised laboratory exercises, and prepared himself with the help of Hitt's *Manual for the Solution of Military Ciphers* for the next lot of lessons to the class. Thus he had an even shorter start over his pupils than the great geneticist J. B. S. Haldane, who on returning from the First World War to Oxford, taught physiology, a subject in which, he said, he had "about six weeks' start on (his) future pupils."

"We had a lot of pioneering to do," Mrs. Friedman remembers.

"Literary ciphers may give you the swing of the thing, but they are in no sense scientific. There were no precedents for us to follow. We simply had to roll up our sleeves and chart a new course. We therefore became the learners or students and the teachers and workers all at once, at the same time."

The eighty officers, and the staff who were teaching them, were all housed in the Aurora Hotel, Aurora, Illinois, the nearest sizable hotel to Riverbank, and it was here, outside the entrance, that at the end of the course the Friedmans organized a witty illustration of what enciphering could mean. Under their direction the eighty officers were photographed in two lines on the steps of the hotel. At first glance, the photograph appears of no particular significance. But an acute observer might notice that while some of the men are facing the camera, others are looking sideways. Reading from left to right, the men facing forward represent the "a"s in the biliteral cipher, those seen in profile represent the "b"s. Thus the first five, standing face-on, sideways, face-on, face-on and sideways, represent the letter K. The total of eighty spelt out Bacon's dictum: "Knowledge is power."

Before the first Riverbank training courses were finished the Friedmans had carried out their first assignment for the British. Its results were spectacular, while the notes that the couple kept on the work and on how it was solved give a useful and early illustration of the problems to which they were to devote their lives.

One morning in the autumn of 1917 Colonel Fabyan walked into their office with a tall thickset man whom he introduced as an inspector from London's Scotland Yard. The visitor carried an attaché case from which he produced many hundreds of letters. They were, he explained, the correspondence between nearly two hundred agents, mostly Hindus, who with the aid of Germans were trying to foment a revolution in India. Some of the agents worked in Britain, some in America. The correspondence, parts of which were in plaintext, had been intercepted by the joint efforts of the two countries, and men were already being arrested in the United States. The names of some writers were known, a fact which helped in the work now to start. The bulk of the correspondence consisted of figures whose significance had so far eluded both the cryptographers of Room 40 and those of the Cipher Bureau in Washington. Could Colonel Fabyan's team help; or, more accurately, could the Friedmans help?

The initial work was carried out by Elizebeth Friedman, who sorted the correspondence into three groups, which she correctly decided had been enciphered or encoded in three different ways. One group of letters consisted of a succession of five-digit numbers such as 38425 24736 47575. In the second group the message consisted of figures — 78–5–48 35–9–17 for instance — with the central figure being frequently repeated. In the third group the numbers — 1–2–7 2–1–16 — contained many single-digit numbers while in each case the central number was either 1 or 2.

The letters written in five-digit numbers were tackled first. By a combination of instinct and experience the Friedmans decided that these had been written in what cryptographers call a pure cipher method using a keyword. To break it they first rewrote the five-digit groups into pairs of digits — 38 42 52 47 36 instead of 38425 and 24736. Next, these two-digit numbers were carefully studied for repetitions, and the mathematical relations existing between these repetitions used to suggest the length of the keyword. It soon became clear that the keyword was probably of four letters and the text was then regrouped, the first, fifth and ninth two-digit numbers being listed together, second, sixth, tenth listed together, and so on. Each list of numbers now represented letters in the alphabet; but in each list the same letter would, due to the introduction of a letter in the four-letter keyword, be represented by a different number, the result being what could be described as four different alphabets. Fitting the letters in each to the numbers in each of the four lists was a comparatively easy task once the principles of frequency were applied.

These principles, part of the solid pemmican feeding crypt-analytic work, deal with the fact that in each language some letters of the alphabet are used more frequently than others, whether the text they make up deals with a love affair or a pitched battle. The tables showing which letters are used more than others differ for different languages. And although there is a general resemblance between tables for the principal west European languages such as English, French, German, Spanish and Italian, the differences between them are enough to suggest which language any particular letter is written in. A message lacking "q"s, for instance, is unlikely to be written in Spanish since the word "que" is common in it. A message written in German will probably reflect the very high frequency of "e"s and "n"s. Each language thus has its own semantic fingerprint and in this case it seemed almost certain that the messages were written in German. Assuming this, it was quickly discovered that the letter "a" was represented by 36 in the first alphabet, by 22 in the second, and so on. From this point it was a short step to reconstruct not only the message but the method by which it had been enciphered.

The initial values of the letters to be enciphered were provided, it was found, from the coordinates of the small square occupied by each letter in the following diagram:

```
  1 2 3 4 5 6 7
1 A B C D E F G
2 H I J K L M N
3 O P Q R S T U
4 V W X Y Z
```

Thus the message COME AT ONCE would first be written as:

49

$$13 — 31 — 26 — 15 — 11 — 36 — 31 — 27 — 13 — 15$$

Next the numerical values of the chosen keyword, which Friedman discovered was in this case LAMP, were added to the original figures. The figures for LAMP, obtained from the square, were 25 — 11 — 26 — 32, which were added thus to the message:

C	O	M	E	A	T	O	N	C	E
13 —	31 —	26 —	15 —	11 —	36—	31 —	27 —	13 —	15
25 —	11 —	26 —	32—	25 —	11	— 26 —	32 —	25 —	11

$$38 — 42 — 52 — 47 — 36 — 47 — 57 — 59 — 38 — 26$$

Broken up into five-digit groups, the message would then be written as 38425 24736 47575 93826.

The second group of messages in the correspondence were different in two ways. They used a system which involved groups of figures, each group containing three separate figures; and the letters were sprinkled with what were obviously unciphered words of plaintext. One long message for instance began with the word "Dear" followed by a string of six figure-groups. Then came "Am back from," followed by five figure-groups and then the two words "Had lots" followed by seven figure-groups. This, Friedman believed, could be nothing but a cipher built up by taking an individual letter from some ordinary book and then indicating it by giving the page on which it was to be found, the line in which it was to be found, and its numerical position in the line. And surely it would be essential to know what the book was before the message could be deciphered? Friedman decided otherwise.

"Look at the groups after the words "HAD LOTS," he later

explained. "The writer has obviously just returned from some place where he "had lots" of — what? Let us assume TROUBLE. If we assume that the word is TROUBLE, then:

$$22 — 7 — 6 \ \ = \ \ T$$
$$22 — 7 — 7 \ \ = \ \ R$$
$$22 — 7 — 10 \ = \ \ O$$
$$22 — 7 — 8 \ \ = \ \ U$$
$$22 — 7 — 14 \ = \ \ B$$
$$22 — 7 — 12 \ = \ \ L$$
$$22 — 7 — 9 \ \ = \ \ E$$

"And, if this is true, does it not follow that in the *book* on page 22, line 7, beginning with the 6th letter, there should be the following:

	6	7	8	9	10	11	12	13	14
Page 22, line 7,	T	R	U	E	O		L		B

"The word TRUE stands out: we may speculate as to what follows it in the book! How about TRUE OF? If that is correct, then we have a new value, $22 — 7 — 11$ equals F!"

But "$22 — 7 — 11$" appears elsewhere in the message and enables the cryptanalyst to produce another almost completed word, F ? U L T, in which the missing letter, represented by $22 — 7 — 13$ in the message, is almost certainly A. This in turn allows the seventh line of page 22 to be read from the sixth letter on as TRUE OF LAB . . . Here LABOR is a justifiable speculation and this provides two more values, since $22 — 7 — 15$ as well as $22 — 7 — 10$ now equals O and $22 — 7 — 16$ equals R. Adding a letter to the decipherment provided a word to add to the book and this in turn provided one or more values to add to the decipherment.

"Had this particular Hindu not been so lazy," Friedman later wrote, "had he not left what he thought were unimportant words in plain English, had he not taken letters close to one another in the book, the job would not have been so easy. In fact had he been quite careful and skipped hither and yon throughout the whole book, never taking more than a single letter or two from a line, we would never have solved the message. But he was careless, and he was lazy, and he left us plenty of clues — so that we could eventually read practically all of the messages without even knowing what book had been used."

By this time, moreover, Friedman and his wife had many clues to the nature of the book. When they had finished the decipherment they had built up about fifty words or phrases which they knew were contained in it. These included CHARLEMAGNE, KAISER, FOREIGN OFFICE, GERMANY, RUSHED TO A NEWSPAPER OFFICE and HISTORICALLY, as well as TRUE OF LABOR. In addition they knew the places in the book where these words and phrases appeared. There seemed little doubt that it dealt with political economy or history, probably as far as these concerned Germany and the Germans.

Despite the decipherment, roughly 95 percent complete, it would obviously be of great use to have the book available at the coming trial of the first fifty Hindus which was to be held in Chicago. Fabyan set to work, inquiring of booksellers throughout the United States if they could trace a book of the required character which had, for instance, the phrase TRUE OF LABOR on the seventh line of the twenty-second page. He had no luck.

However, the luck was not necessary. Shortly before the trial opened in Chicago, the Hindu who had written the message was confronted with the solution. He saw that it was correct, broke down, confessed, and then named the book he had used: Price Collier's *Germany and the Germans*. Friedman, called to Chicago to give evidence, made a hurried visit to the biggest bookshop in the city, discovered the book, and confirmed that the decipherment had been correct.

The third method used by the Hindus — a code and not a cipher — gave itself away by the use of the figures 1 or 2 in the center of each group, a plain indication that a two-column book, probably a dictionary, had been used, with each word of the encoded message being given by the page number of the book, the column number of the page and then the position of the word in the column. Once again the Friedmans turned for help to the frequency principle. This time, however, it was the principle as applied not to letters alone but to whole words. Just how great a help the frequency principle can be is suggested by one analysis of written texts totaling 100,000 words. While these included 10,161 different words, 10 words made up 26,677 of the 100,000; 100 made up 54,303, and 1,000 made up 78,336. Such an analysis, moreover, was known to be correct for any sizable number of words. "The," "of," "and," "to," "a," "in," "that," "it," "is" and "I" are, in that order, the most frequent words, a fact which enabled Friedman at least to begin decoding the messages. But word frequency gives an additional help when the code is based on a dictionary, since it is known that in English, for instance, words beginning with A form 6.43 percent of those used, words beginning with B form 5.25 percent, words beginning with C form 9.82 percent and so on. Comparable percentages are of course known for other languages. Thus once the percentage-use of any code number has been worked out, it is possible to say that it probably begins with one particular letter. "Again," Friedman has pointed out in describing this particular case, "suppose it has been definitely established that the code number 97–2–14 represents the word YOU: the code number 99–2–17, which may occur several times, must represent a word, certainly not far beyond YOU, and since there are but two or three relatively uncommon words (YOUNG, YOUTH, etc.) intervening between YOU and YOUR, the word is probably YOUR."

53

Working along these lines, more than 90 percent of the third group of messages was worried out. But, as in the earlier case, the book used was still unknown, even though the page, column and position of many words had been determined. This was still the position when, in December, 1917, Friedman traveled to San Francisco to give evidence as another 130 conspirators were tried. Here, waiting to be called, he continued his search for the elusive dictionary, but still without success. Then, in the University of California at Berkeley, he met on the campus a former colleague from Cornell. "Why not try the college bookshop?" his friend asked.

In the bookshop the two men at first had no luck. Then a very elderly member of the staff asked them to wait for a minute. He retired into the dim recesses of the shop and returned a few minutes later with the second volume of an English-German dictionary published in 1880. Friedman had to check only a few references before he knew that this was the volume.

As in the previous trial in Chicago, the evidence in San Francisco was vastly strengthened by Friedman's ability to produce a copy of the actual volume which had been used by the conspirators. But it was a sensational trial for another reason. One of the Hindus had turned state's evidence and was in the witness-box when another conspirator produced a revolver from beneath his robes and shot his compatriot dead. The shot was answered by another as a state marshal at the rear of the court fired over the heads of the public to kill the murderer.

Here, with a state witness shot at least as a partial result of purely theoretical evidence, it is appropriate to ask the question regularly raised throughout Friedman's career by his noncryptological friends. When a message has been deciphered, how is it possible to know that the decipherment is correct?

There are, he would always explain, two equally important elements in any judgment about the validity of a decipherment. One is the validity of the plaintext itself, the second is the validity of the key by which it was obtained. The first is simple enough, since the deciphered text has merely to conform intelligibly, in technical or grammatical construction, with the language in which it is supposedly written. "The cryptanalyst," he would go on to say, "will accept as *mechanically* or semantically valid whatever statement comes out, so long as the statement is structurally sound as regards the elements which compose it and the sequences in which they appear."

Testing the validity of the key is not quite so cut-and-dried and consists, basically, of applying the theory of probabilities. If a key could have come into being only once in a billion times according to the laws of chance, then it is reasonable to assume that such a key is no accident but the result of conscious manipulation. Alternatively, if it is found that according to the laws of chance the key could be formed by sheer accident nine out of ten times, then not much faith should be put in it.

The solution of the Hindu ciphers gave a boost to Riverbank's reputation in Washington. But Fabyan, a shrewd man, appreciated that this reputation sprang largely from the cryptographic team headed by Friedman and his wife and he decided to hang on to that team as long as possible. He was therefore perturbed when a note from Washington warned him that Friedman was liable to be called up, should obviously be commissioned, and would probably be best employed as a cryptanalyst on General Pershing's staff in France. Not at all, the colonel replied. If the young Friedman were to be called up and commissioned then he should surely remain at Riverbank, doing the work at which he had become so expert. But, he went on, were it really necessary, then surely it would be possible for him to be "appointed a Vice-Consul, unassigned, with the understanding that he is to stay here and be loaned to such duties as may appear to be in the best interests of the Government. If this is non-consistent," the colonel went on, "perhaps the Attorney-General would consider appointing him a professional witness for the Department of Justice, or (another official) would consider appointing him a special investigator. . . ."

Whatever the reaction of the authorities in Washington to these extraordinary suggestions, they were waiting for a reply from Friedman. For while they had written to Fabyan, they had also written directly to Friedman offering him a commission. However, no reply came. The reason was simple. Fabyan had made a regular practice of opening his staff's letters and this one never reached its destination. The situation might have worked to Friedman's discredit had he not himself already been making efforts to join the Signal Corps. Eventually he succeeded, but not before he and his wife had performed a feat which may, quite literally, have saved the lives of some thousands of Allied troops.

Chapter Four

Cryptography at War

E ARLY IN 1918 the British decided that an adaptation of an earlier enciphering device should be used in the field by both the British and the American forces. This was the cryptograph, consisting of two concentric rings of letters with an "hour hand" pointing to one ring and a "minute hand" pointing to the other. The letters could be disposed according to any prearranged choice and when one of the hands was pointed to the plaintext letter the other hand, to which the first was geared as in a clock, pointed to an enciphering letter. The device was known as the Wheatstone cryptograph after Sir Charles Wheatstone, the British scientist best known for his invention of the Wheatstone bridge for measuring electrical resistance. Wheatstone was for years believed to have been the first to think of this enciphering method and it was only between the two World Wars that Friedman found it to have been foreshadowed by Decius Wadsworth, the U.S. Army's first chief of ordnance in 1817, more than sixty years previously.

The cryptograph had for long been considered too easily deciphered for practical use. However, a member of British Intelligence, Captain St. Vincent Plett, had ingeniously developed from the Wheatstone cryptograph two eccentric circles of letters, one of which contained twenty-seven intervals, and the other twenty-six. The device was first tested by the French, who claimed it to be unbreakable for all practicable purposes. The British Army then tested it and Captain Frank Moorman, head of the American cryptographic services at General Pershing's headquarters, reported: "British officers claim that solution of messages sent by it is possible only with a great many messages and that so long a time will be required that messages will lose their value before solution." The only fear about its use in the field, he went on, was that if it were captured by the Germans they would be able to make use of it and "we would be unable to read their messages."

Thousands of the Plett invention had been made and issued. There seemed no reason why they should not be used operationally but the Cipher Bureau in Washington suggested that as a final check their security should be tested by the Riverbank team. Six short messages, averaging only forty letters in length were therefore sent down from Washington.

"It looked like an insurmountable task," Mrs. Friedman recalls. "A field cipher, used in war, would be utilized a hundred or two hundred times a day, and even if the key were changed every day, there would be a great mass of messages to study. But here we had six short messages and we were dealing with two alphabets; one moving irregularly against the other and we had no knowledge of either."

Friedman lined up the short enciphered texts and began to puzzle them out. His only hope was to assume parts of the text and then attempt to build up an alphabet or at least part of one. After two hours he believed that he had the basis of the alphabet on the outer disc.

This half of the solution had come from assuming that the person enciphering the message in Washington had been unwise enough to use as a key the word "cipher." The chance of this happening had first come to Friedman's notice when, a few months earlier, the wife of Captain Parker Hitt had visited the Riverbank Laboratories. Her husband, whose *Manual* had been used by the Friedmans in training the War Department classes, had invented an enciphering device based on the use of sliding paper strips and Mrs. Hitt hoped that the Riverbank team would find unbreakable a message enciphered with it. "I solved the message by guessing the key Mrs. Hitt employed," Friedman later said. "She wasn't wise to the quirks of inexperienced cryptographic clerks; she used RIVERBANK LABORATORIES as the key, just as I suspected she would."

Now, dealing with the Plett device, Friedman argued that if the encipherer had been foolish enough to use as a key one word concerned with the enciphering process, then he might have used something similar as a basis for the second alphabet. For nearly an hour, he tested a variety of "matching" words. Then he appealed to Elizebeth Friedman.

"I was sitting across the room from him, busily engaged on another message," she has said. "He asked me to lean back in my chair, close my eyes and make my mind blank, at least as blank as possible. Then he would ask me a question. I was not to consider the reply even for a second but just give the word which his question brought to my mind. I did as he said. He spoke the word 'cipher' and I instantly replied: 'Machine.' A few minutes later he said the answer was right."

Shortly afterwards the plaintext of all the messages, the first reading: "This message is absolutely indecipherable," was being telegraphed to Washington. The next day General Churchill, head of Army Intelligence in Washington, telegraphed to London: "Please inform Captain Hay of British Military Intelligence that messages enciphered by Plett's machine have been broken by method of attack different from any considered by inventor, and that system is considered dangerous in presence of enemy."

One interesting point in the nobbling of the device, whose use would have presented considerable danger and could have caused great loss of life, is Friedman's failure to think of the word "machine" which his wife had produced with automatic response. He had tried words such as "alphabet," "indecipherable," "solution," "system" and "method." But it had not occurred to his meticulous mind that a small hand-operated device could be considered a machine.

Shortly after solving the Plett messages Friedman was drawn into what was almost certainly the first argument over the safety of enciphered messages sent by teleprinter. Two years earlier the American Telephone and Telegraph Company had been involved in the extension of their teleprint services for defense purposes. As with virtually all such services, the means adopted was the Baudot Code which — like Bacon's biliteral cipher — uses permutations of two different elements, taken in groups of five, to represent the characters of the alphabet. But instead of Bacon's "a"s or "b"s, the electric teleprinter could contrast the presence or absence of current. A paper tape in which there were groups of up to five holes transverse to the length of the tape, each group representing a letter of the alphabet, was fed into the sending teleprinter. The current, uninterrupted where there were holes in the tape, produced a similar tape on a receiving teleprinter at the other end of the line and from this tape the original message could be transcribed.

In the winter of 1917–1918 an A.T.&T. employee, Gilbert Vernam, proposed an ingenious and apparently safe way of enciphering such messages. All that was necessary, he claimed, was to feed into the sending teleprinter not only the tape bearing the message but, at the same time, a second tape bearing a number of key characters. At the other end of the line a tape identical to that bearing the key characters was fed into the receiving teleprinter; the impulses it produced combined with the impulses being received to give a tape bearing the original message; but — the whole object of the exercise — the message being transmitted between the two points would be "scrambled" by the second tape with the key characters, and would therefore be indecipherable to anyone who succeeded in tapping the line.

The combining rule for these operations disclosed in Vernam's patent was one in which a symbol in the message plus a similar symbol in the key produced one of the two available elements and in which a symbol in the message plus a dissimilar symbol in the key produced the other. Diagrammatically it can be shown thus:

Message character	+ + − − −
Key	+ − − + +
Cipher character	+ − + − −
Key	+ − − + +
Deciphered character	+ + − − −

However, it was recognized that the opposite rule would work equally well, with two dissimilar elements giving a plus, and two similar elements giving a minus.

As well as being safe, this method had the enormous advantage that both ciphering and enciphering was carried out automatically. It was realized, however, that if a line over which such messages were being sent was tapped by an enemy and if, furthermore, a sufficient number of messages were recorded, then a cryptanalyst just might be able to decipher them. But ease of decipherment is very closely linked with the number of messages in any one system which can be studied. The greater the number, the less difficult the job. Another A.T.&T. employee, L. F. Morehouse, therefore proposed an ingenious but simple method by which the key was automatically changed. This involved the use for enciphering not of one tape but of two, one having 1,000 characters and the other having 999. The tapes were geared together to produce a third tape as the key, and since the relevant positions of the first and the second tapes could be changed one character at a time, the key tape would not be repeated until 999,000 characters had been processed, the equivalent of about 160,000 words.

In the spring of 1918, three circuits using this presumably secure method were opened. All ran from Washington and proceeded separately to New York; Hoboken, New Jersey; and Norfolk, Virginia; and all carried extremely important information about troop movements. Then the Signal Corps, which had already approved the system, began to have doubts. The almost inevitable question was asked. What did the Riverbank people think about the system's security?

In May, 1918, Fabyan and Friedman arrived in the A.T.&T's New York offices to watch a demonstration. "They seemed impressed," says R. D. Parker, then head of the company's telegraph section, "but requested permission to have a private discussion. They retired to one corner of the office and after a whispered consultation stated that they thought messages enciphered as we had described it could be broken."

Later, Friedman revealed what it was that was worrying him: the fact that the slightest carelessness by anyone entrusted with the actual enciphering would lay open to easy solution all the messages by means of the same key. "Since carelessness on the part of the personnel to be entrusted with the operation of the machine, and ignorance on their part for the reasons of every precaution necessary in cipher work are to be expected," he added, "the existence of this opening for an attack must be admitted." In addition, he went on, even if there were no error through carelessness, the mechanics of the machine, and certain features of the system, made such an attack "not only practicable, but easy under normal conditions."

In view of the doubts raised by Fabyan and Friedman, it was agreed that a series of test messages should be sent by A.T.&T. to Riverbank. But it was June 11, 1918, before they arrived and by this time Friedman had already left for France, having ignored Fabyan's injunction to stay and joined up in the normal way in Washington.

It was less than three years since he had gone to Riverbank as a geneticist and even less since he had taken his first steps in cryptography. Yet during this brief period he had already begun to change the attitude with which the subject was regarded. Hitherto, cryptography had been thought of as a slightly occult science. Frequency principles had for long been employed, and there were other examples of a scientific and orderly approach to deciphering the apparently undecipherable. Friedman, however, had from the first tackled the problems of the subject as a researcher in a laboratory, anxious to investigate them with any of the mathematical or statistical tools available although willing to admit that the good logical approach might always be improved by a dash of illogical intuition. He had, moreover, begun to give fresh sinew to the literature of the subject. When America entered the First World War it was not only cryptographers who were in short supply. Information that could be gleaned from printed material consisted of little more than Parker Hitt's *Manual,* and a very brief paper by Captain Mauborgne on a method of solving messages enciphered by the Wheatstone cryptograph. There were also the two or three articles by Edgar Allan Poe, and it is revealing of the then state of the art that it is necessary to cite the journalism, written nearly three-quarters of a century earlier, of a novelist who was, despite his other virtues, a not-very-good amateur cryptographer.

Friedman had begun to fill this wasteland in 1917 with a short paper: "A Method of Reconstructing the Primary Alphabet from a Single One of the Series of Secondary Alphabets." It explained, in comparatively simple terms, how study of the spatial relationships among the letters of the secondary alphabets — the method used to solve the first of the three Hindu systems — could lead to reconstruction of the primary alphabet. It was his first paper on cryptology and it is of historical importance since it pointed out one of the directions in which the cryptanalysis of complex ciphers could be simplified and expedited.

It was followed early in 1918 by seven more papers, one written in collaboration with Mrs. Friedman, and each marking some fresh innovation in cryptographic literature. Thus one described methods of solving ciphers which used as the key a long continuous text, or "running key" — and on the original Friedman pinned a note to Fabyan: "It was said as recently as three months ago, 'It can't be done' or 'It is very questionable.' "

These papers were the foundations on which the huge edifice of twentieth century cryptology was very largely to be built. Known as the Riverbank Publications, they were copyrighted by Fabyan, who paid for their publication. Of most, only some two hundred copies were printed. They have since become bookselling rarities, and the air of mystery surrounding them is deepened by the fact that in most cases they failed to carry the author's name.

Friedman had thus started to lay the foundations of his career when he crossed the Atlantic and in July, 1918, reported for duty with Military Intelligence at General Pershing's headquarters in Chaumont. Officially, the group was known as the Radio Intelligence Section but this was merely a cover name for the German Code and Cipher Solving Section of the General Staff. In addition to separate sections working on codes and ciphers respectively there were other groups concentrating on direction-finding and traffic analysis. The main bulk of encoded or enciphered messages

64

was already being sent by wireless and even when such messages could not be decoded or deciphered their volume alone could often provide information. Direction-finders could reveal the places from which messages were being sent, while the ebb and flow of enemy wireless traffic could itself betray enemy intentions.

On reporting for duty to Colonel Frank Moorman, the head of the complete unit, Friedman was given the choice of joining either the cipher section or the code section. His choice is a small, but early and revealing, indication of the hold which the subject already had on him. "Having had considerable experience with the solution of the former types of cryptosystems but none with the latter," he later explained, "and being desirous of gaining such experience, I asked to be assigned to the code-solving unit, in order to broaden my professional knowledge and practice in cryptology. Little did I realise what a painful and frustrating period of learning and training I had undertaken, but my choice turned out to be a very wise and useful one."

The Germans had by this time abandoned the existing idea that code-books were impractical for tactical communication use in the combat zone and were using two types of field code. One was called the Schluesselheft, known to the Americans as the "three-number code"; the other was the Satzbuch or "three-letter code." The first was a small standardized code containing 1,000 frequently used words, expressions, digits and letters, each having as code equivalent a three-digit number. A two-part key was used for enciphering and deciphering three numbers, and each German division on the Western Front compiled and issued its own key.

Although the Schluesselheft was ready by January, 1918, it was not issued until March 10, the opening day of the last great German offensive that was expected to drive the Allies back to the Channel coast. However, shortly after midnight an American intercept station picked up one of the first messages to be sent in the new code. Soon afterwards, the station to which the message had been sent radio ed a brief reply incorporating the letters OS, the current German abbreviation for *ohne Sinn* or "message unintelligible." The OS was followed by two message-groups known to be from an earlier code which had been partly broken. Then came a repetition of the first message; but this time it was sent in the old code so that the Americans now had the same message sent in both the code which they had already broken and the new code which had been introduced only a few hours earlier. "These solutions," Friedman wrote in a later history of the German Army's use of field codes, "were telegraphed immediately to the French Code Office. We had not as yet adopted a method of secret communication by telegraph with the British Code Office, and it may be interesting to note that to add to the dramatic situation these solutions were despatched to the British by a special aeroplane." The sending of this one message, Colonel Moorman later commented, "must certainly have cost the lives of thousands of Germans and conceivably it changed the result of one of the greatest efforts made by the German armies."

More difficult than day-to-day work on the Schluesselheft were attempts to find a solution for the Satzbuch or three-letter code. "In the first place," Friedman has said, "it had a much larger vocabulary, with nulls and many variants for frequently used words, letters, syllables and numbers; in the second place, and what constituted the real stumbling block to solution, was the fact that it was a true two-part randomized or "hatted" code; and in the third place, each sector of the front used a different edition of the code, so that traffic not only had to be identified as to the sector to which it belonged but also it was not possible to combine all the messages for the purpose of building up frequencies of usage of code groups." So good was the German Satzbuch that after the first American attempts to devise their own code-books, they decided to scrap the lot and base their work on the German method.

Friedman came late into this American effort in France, a fact which rankled with him for years. Nevertheless he did play a significant part in the later history of one of the most famous field ciphers in military history. This was the ADFGVX cipher, also introduced by the Germans for the first time at the start of their great March offensive in 1918. Restricted to use by the German High Command, it could be expected to contain information of more importance than that in the Schluesselheft. But the number of messages sent in ADFGVX was comparatively small, from about 25 a day when it was first introduced up to about 150 a day at the end of two months. In addition the cipher, which at first used only the five letters, A, D, F, G and X, appeared to be unbreakable. The procedure was simple: a message would be enciphered, one letter at a time, by writing two cipher letters for each letter in the plaintext so that the complete encipherment had double the number of letters in the plaintext. The next step was to separate these pairs of letters and mix them in accordance with a prearranged key which was changed every day. Thus the system involved a substitution, a division, and finally a transposition. "In brief," Friedman has said,

"there were in those days three and only three different methods of attacking that cipher. Under the first method it was necessary to find, as the first step, two or more messages with identical plain-text beginnings because they could be used to uncover the transposition, which was the second step. Once this had been done, the cryptanalyst then had to deal with a substitution cipher in which two-letter combinations of the letters A, D, F, G, V and X represented single plain-text letters. The messages were usually of sufficient length for this purpose. Under the second method, two or more messages with identical plain-text endings could be used to uncover the transposition. This was easier even than in the case of messages with identical beginnings. You might think that cases of

67

messages with identical beginnings or endings would be
rather rare, but the addiction to stereotypic phraseology
was so prevalent in all German military communications
that there were almost invariably found, in each day's
traffic, messages with similar beginnings or endings, and
sometimes both. Under the third method of solution it was
necessary to find several messages with exactly the same
number of letters. This happened, but not often.

It took about a month before the French cryptanalyst, Captain
Georges Painvin, succeeded in working out a method of tackling
the cipher. Then, early in April, the interception of two messages
with identical groups enabled him to provide the key to the cipher
used on that particular day. Another solution followed later in the
month. But by the end of June the keys for only ten different days
had been found. "Yet," Friedman has said, "because the traffic on
those days was very heavy, about 50% of all messages ever sent in
that cipher, from its inception to its discard, were read, and a great
deal of valuable intelligence was derived from them. On one occasion solution was so rapid that an important German operation
disclosed by one message was completely frustrated."

Many years later Colonel Moorman wrote a note crediting
Friedman with the solution, but on it Friedman himself wrote the
comment: "I wish I could accept the credit — but my only connection with the ADFGVX cipher was to originate a mechanical
method for solution, given two messages with similar endings.
Painvin deserves all the credit." Friedman was rarely over-modest
but it seems that here he rather belittled the method which he
worked out after the end of the war. It is described in a short note
dated January 6, 1919, which ends with the comment that it is
"almost entirely a mechanical one, and may save time in determining the transposition-key in this cipher."

When the war ended in November, 1918, Friedman had spent

only five months at General Pershing's headquarters. Yet he had already picked up a huge amount of practical knowledge about the ways in which codes — and to some extent ciphers — are used in the field. This is clear from a technical paper "Field Codes Used by the German Army During the World War" which he wrote on the orders of Colonel Moorman during the first weeks of 1919. It also contains many indications of how he himself had gone about his job, as when he describes the first steps in breaking a code. "It should be noted," he says, "that in this whole process the part played by chance, by the happy coincidences which were always lurking everywhere for the watchful eye of the worker to note, by the mistakes of a foolish or a careless encoder, and by a fortunate 'long shot' or guess by the decoder, cannot be over-estimated. Often the minutest and most insignificant of clues formed the starting point for the unravelling of a whole chain of groups." He explained how the expert decoder begins to recognize the relative positions of groups in messages, even though he cannot yet understand them, and how a change of code will make itself apparent to the expert even by the change in spatial relationships of familiar groups.

His almost instinctive "feel" for the operations of the cryptographer on the other side of the hill, a form of intuition which was to be one of Friedman's strengths two decades later, was paralleled by his noting of the enemy weaknesses which helped cryptanalysis, weaknesses which were to be noted again during the Second World War. The German operators, he commented, often showed what he called an unintelligent pedantry, failing to alter the form or punctuation of messages and thereby helping the cryptanalyst. They also made a habit of sending proverbs as practice messages. "Adding to this," he said, "the fact that the German had a predilection for repeating certain proverbs many times caused the establishment of a single letter often to result in locating these proverbs and thus, in turn, the solution of a whole series of important spelling groups in a new code was effected."

This practical experience was doubly important. It not only supplemented the theoretical work on which Friedman had been engaged at Riverbank but was experience which had been gained by only a small handful of men. However, with demobilization coming nearer, he had to make an important decision: should he return to the Riverbank Laboratories and serve once again under the dictatorial overlordship of Colonel Fabyan, by now well inflated with success and already wondering what decoration or honor he was to receive for his war services?

Whatever the counterbalancing attractions of Riverbank, one thing made Friedman loath to return. For in France, during his contacts with senior officers, he learned for the first time how Washington had wanted to commission him early in 1917. That there was something more to his reaction than dislike of his employer's double-dealing was made clear in a note which H. O. Yardley of the Cipher Bureau wrote to General Churchill, the director of Military Intelligence, when Friedman's future was subsequently being discussed. "He feels," wrote Yardley, "that he missed one of the big opportunities of his life by not being commissioned in 1917, for had he been sent to France at that time he would have had an opportunity to make a name for himself."

However, Friedman was quite confident of his own abilities and powers, and rarely happy unless deploying them fully. Therefore his reply to a bombardment of letters from Fabyan, appealing for his return when he came out of uniform, was distinctly frosty. It was also detailed, running to more than four single-spaced typed pages. He first upbraided Fabyan for concealing the offer from Washington, then pointed out that neither Elizebeth Friedman nor he had any particular wish to return to Riverbank; and it proceeded, in the bluntest possible way, to criticize Fabyan's running of his laboratories. "Honesty," Friedman wrote, "prompts me to say that in my opinion your judgment of human nature and ability along academic lines will have to undergo severe changes to enable you to make a success of academic activities, as you have of business activities. I will also add that the methods and judgments by means of which you attained success in the commercial world, in my opinion, will not, and can not attain success in the academic world." Then, after lambasting the colonel for trying to claim the existence of an apparently nonexistent biliteral cipher in Shakespeare, he concluded: "This letter will reach you through Elizebeth. If there are any statements to which she objects she may amend them or make such comment as she sees fit."

To all this, Colonel Fabyan replied loftily and briefly. "The facts in the case are that you are practically loaned for the emergency," he wrote. "That emergency no longer exists and in justice to yourself, your own future, and myself, I think the sooner you return to Riverbank, the better."

For some while that seemed very unlikely. Friedman wrote the history of the Army's Code and Cipher Solving Branch, returned to the United States, and was demobilized on April 5, 1919. His wife, who had left Riverbank in the autumn of 1918 and returned to her family home in Huntington, now joined him in New York. Together they visited the Friedman family in Pittsburgh.

Then began the search for a job. Despite his fascination with cryptography Friedman still hankered after genetics. It had, of course, been his first love. But there is more than a suspicion that even by 1919 he had begun to sense the devious paths down which he could be drawn by cryptography, the ambiguities of ethics that were eventually to riddle the work, and the situation which years later would cause him to hold his head in his hands and mutter of his cryptographic work in Intelligence: "How on earth did I get into this business." Whatever the strength of these feelings in 1919, it was as a geneticist that Friedman now applied to a succession of companies in and around New York. But industry had not yet come to appreciate genetics. "When I arrived from France," he wrote to Yardley in mid-May, "my mind was fully made up to go into business. After looking around for a considerable length of time, and conferring with friends, it seemed inadvisable to do so just at present on account of unsettled business conditions."

Meanwhile, Colonel Fabyan was keeping up the pressure. More than once he cabled, "Your salary has been continuing," and implied that it would be waiting when the prodigal returned to Riverbank. And he would, it appeared, be happy to welcome back both the Friedmans on their own terms. Eventually, they succumbed.

First, however, they laid down four conditions: they would not live on the estate, under Fabyan's eagle eye; they would brook no interference from the colonel in their private lives; they must be given absolute freedom to prove, or to disprove, the existence in Shakespeare of the biliteral cipher. And their names must appear on anything they wrote.

The outcome was that Fabyan finally agreed, and the summer of 1919 thus found the Friedmans back, although this time with a difference. They rented a small furnished house on the outskirts of Geneva, led their own lives independently of the Riverbank community and at first seemed likely to settle down comfortably. Two things eventually combined to alter that prospect: a steady deterioration in relations with Fabyan, as reluctant as ever to look objectively at the possibilities of the biliteral cipher, and ever-stronger suggestions from Washington that the Friedmans would be better off in cryptological service there. Even so, it was to be some eighteen months before the question of their future was finally resolved: a year and a half divided between what they increasingly saw as futile work with Mrs. Gallup, and the more exciting cryptographic work which was still pushed their way from Washington.

They had been back at Riverbank only a few weeks when they received from Major Mauborgne the first twenty-five letters of each of twenty-five messages enciphered by a system he had adapted from the paper-strip device which Parker Hitt's wife had unsuccessfully brought to Riverbank in 1917. The paper strips had now been replaced by twenty-six heavy brass discs on the edges of which the letters of the alphabet were engraved in twenty-six specially assorted sequences, and it was the encipherment of messages with these that Friedman was now being asked to solve. So was Yardley, now a major, at the Cipher Bureau. Neither Friedman nor Yardley had any success. "Nobody ever solved the messages, even after a good deal of work and even after Mauborgne told us that two consecutive words in one of the challenge messages were the words 'are you,' " Friedman later admitted.

Following the failure of both Yardley and Friedman to solve the test messages, Mauborgne proposed to the army that the device should be brought into official use. At this point, Friedman was asked to comment, and in view of the sequel, it is significant that he still remained cautious about the security of the device.

"I stated," he later wrote, "that while the thing in my opinion was not indecipherable by any means, despite the failure of everybody to solve Mauborgne's test messages, I believed the cipher to be much superior to anything the Army had yet had along that line, and that it would do for the purposes for which it was intended. I think it would hold the enemy from three to thirty hours under the best of conditions. The technical committee met a few weeks [later] and it was not in their province to decide upon the merits in a scientific way as to indecipherability and they naturally did not need me. At any rate, I was going to get myself on record in some way. I don't want the time to come when somebody will pop up and say I approved without reservations."

Mauborgne eventually went ahead with the device which became Cipher Device M-94 and was used for a decade not only by the U.S. Armed Forces but by the U.S. Coast Guard and the Intelligence agencies of the U.S. Treasury, apparently without loss of security. Nevertheless, Friedman's caution had been justified, a fact that he discovered years later when, in a dusty file in Mauborgne's former office, he found the plaintexts of the messages, whose first letters he had been given in enciphered form. The first two were: "Phenols are benzole derivati(ves)" and "Xylonite and artificial ivor(y)," and the rest consisted of similarly unusual and exotic words. Both Friedman and Yardley had assumed that the challenges would contain words of the sort normally found in military messages for which the enciphering device had been perfected. Had they done so, the test messages would very probably have been broken.

These almost deliberately misleading tests had naturally raised in Friedman's mind the cryptographic question as to whether an unbreakable cipher was a real possibility. He always maintained that Edgar Allan Poe's statement, that an unsolvable cipher could never be devised, had to be qualified in two ways. "It is possible," he once said "to write in a comparatively simple manner a single message which will remain unread. That is because a very short message does not give the experts enough to work on. On the other hand with a sufficient volume of text available for study, a cipher system that cannot be broken down has not yet been found in practical military or diplomatic correspondence. If enough messages in a particular cipher are available, it is safe to say that no system is absolutely unconquerable." The situation was to be further qualified toward the end of his life as some of the largest computers in the world began to be used by the National Security Agency. These huge machines had never, Friedman always insisted, been of use in breaking codes or ciphers. He was, however, careful not to deny that they could, in the first place, be used for devising the unbreakable.

While he was still at work on Mauborgne's test messages he became, as he put it, "an interested party in a rather warm argument conducted by letters exchanged between Colonel Fabyan, the Chief Signal Officer, the Director of Military Intelligence, and the War Department." The argument concerned the security of the

A.T.&T. encipherment system which he and Fabyan had inspected in New York more than a year previously. Following Friedman's departure for France, Fabyan had put a number of the Riverbank staff on to the task of solving the A.T.&T.'s test messages, but without success. Never despondent, he had carried on and as late as March 22, 1919, had written to the company: "I am still of the opinion that the cipher is breakable, although it has cost me several thousand dollars to confirm my off-hand opinion expressed in your office."

He continued to make this claim throughout the early summer: the result, it is difficult not to feel, of his knowledge that Friedman would be coming back to Riverbank. After all, Friedman had always thought that the system could be broken.

The authorities disagreed — not unnaturally, since the system had been carrying sensitive traffic for more than a year — and on August 8, 1919, General Churchill went so far as to sign the following single-sentence letter to the chief signal officer: "The mechanical means of enciphering messages with an arbitrary, meaningless running key of 999,000 letters, provided no two messages are enciphered at the same point on the tape as explained by Major Mauborgne, Signal Corps, and Major Yardley, Military Intelligence Branch, to officials of the American Telegraph and Telephone Company, is considered by this office to be absolutely indecipherable."

To back up the claim, the cipher tapes of about 150 messages selected from a single day's traffic were sent from Washington to Riverbank on October 6. Fabyan now had his Friedman; even so, confidence had been undermined by General Churchill's "absolutely."

For six weeks, sometimes working twelve hours a day, Friedman applied himself to the problem to which, although he may not have known it, the star of his reputation had been attached. He used his staff and towards the end of the operation the staff became discouraged. This, he used to say, was the first time that they had spent such a long time without success. He was still confident that his method of attack was correct; he could not understand what could possibly have gone wrong. Then he had an idea. Some of his friends have called it luck. Others might see it as a tiny flutter of pride mixed with genius, a disbelief that he, of all people, could fail. Was it not possible, he now asked himself, that an error had been made in transcribing the punched tapes into characters on paper? He suggested a check. Before it was finished, one of his assistants discovered that in dealing with the tapes he had completely omitted one character. The single omission came at a crucial point and its restoration allowed an entry into the plaintext to be started.

Within days the system had been broken and on December 8, Fabyan telegraphed the chief signal officer telling him that all the messages had been deciphered. "In order to prove that this was true," Friedman has said, "I sent a perforated cipher-message tape to each of the officers involved. In order to decipher these messages the chief signal officer had to use his own key tapes which had been employed in enciphering the challenge messages, so that Riverbank was in a position to produce the plain-text of any of the latter on request, if further proof of solution was needed or desired."

General Churchill was forced to retract. "Your very brilliant scientific achievement reflects great credit upon you and your whole personnel," he wrote to Fabyan. "It would be impossible to exaggerate in paying you and Riverbank the deserved tribute for this very scholarly accomplishment." The method was abandoned soon afterwards. More significantly, cipher printing telegraphy was virtually forgotten by the Signal Corps for two decades.

Whether Friedman's decipherment of what Churchill had called the "absolutely unbreakable code" was the achievement that made the authorities see his help as essential is not clear. But it was certainly only a month or so later that Washington began to increase the pressure for his recruitment into government service.

Meanwhile, however, Friedman was putting finishing touches to the paper which became the foundation stone of the new cryptography. This was "The Index of Coincidence and Its Applications in Cryptography," a ninety-one-page explanation of how statistical principles and techniques, especially those based upon coincidences in cryptographic texts, could be applied to cryptanalysis, a word which Friedman here used for the first time. While the paper described how two specific cipher systems could be broken, its importance sprang from the fact that the methods described were radically different, and basically more scientific, than those used in the existing state of the art. After "The Index of Coincidence," cryptography would never be the same again.

The manuscript of the paper was handed over to Fabyan in the summer of 1920. For a long while, nothing happened. Then, after Friedman had started work in Washington, two bound copies were sent him by Fabyan. He noticed, with interest, that while his name was given on the cover it was not given on the title page. Stranger still, Friedman discovered two years later that "L'Indice de coincidence et ses applications en cryptographie" had been printed in Paris where it was being generally attributed to General Cartier, the head of the Cryptanalytic Service of the French Army General Staff.

The miserable story came to light only bit by bit. After Friedman's departure Fabyan had sent the manuscript to General Cartier, apparently without giving details of its authorship. Cartier and his colleagues had been so impressed that under some arrangement of which Friedman was never told, the paper was translated and printed without delay. Subsequently Cartier had the original English manuscript printed in Paris and a number of copies sent to Fabyan.

It is at this point that any possibility of honest misunderstanding disappears. For Fabyan, knowing that Friedman would object to the omission of his name from the paper, had stripped a few

French-printed English-language copies of their covers, had fresh covers with Friedman's name on them printed in Chicago and then rebound the copies in the Chicago covers. Two were sent to Friedman who acquired a third copy some years later. None others are known to exist.

However, that skulduggery lay in the future as throughout the autumn of 1920 Friedman considered renewed inducements to leave Riverbank for Washington. As early as April 25, 1919, only a few weeks after demobilization, he had received from Yardley what must have then seemed a cryptic letter. If all went well, Yardley said, he would be able to offer Friedman a commission as a first lieutenant in the regular army, or a salary of $3,000 a year as a civilian. Mrs. Friedman could be offered $1,520, and both appointments would be to a permanent organization which was not specified. Friedman replied within the week, briefly noting that the $3,000 would be acceptable but making no comment on the commission. However, the offer was not confirmed and the Friedmans returned to Riverbank.

On the surface he showed no particular enthusiasm for a Washington job, and his confidence in his own ability to get what he wanted in the end is brought out in two letters to Major Mauborgne, by then in charge of the Signal Corps and making determined efforts to recruit his former colleague. "If Uncle Sam makes me a proposition that is more satisfactory than the one I have, all things considered," he wrote in the first — while skillfully omitting any reference to the agonies of Riverbank — "I will talk it over with Mrs. F., and consider it most carefully. But I wish to say that I am not looking for a job and that had you not written me, it would not even have occurred to me to enter the application."

Uncle Sam made the proposition and Friedman wired a reply by return. "Your letter serious disappointment," it went. "Could not possibly accept lieutenancy. Might consider captaincy. Won't you please lay matter immediately before Chief Signal Officer if you see fit to determine if exception possible in my case. Feel my experience and ability of considerable value to Signal Corps and certainly worth more than lieutenancy. Please consider this confidential and wire reply."

Whether Friedman was persuaded to lower his sights or Uncle Sam was persuaded to increase his offer is not recorded, but shortly afterwards Friedman attended an army medical board. He was turned down, without benefit of appeal, on account of a heart condition. The chairman of the board was a distant relative of Colonel Fabyan and there was for long a suspicion in the Friedman family that the heart condition, if not entirely imaginary, had been given undue importance. Friedman's subsequent attacks, although thirty-five and more years later, suggest that the colonel was probably innocent.

However, Mauborgne was insistent, a way around the regulations was devised, and by November both Friedman and his wife had signed six-month contracts to work as civilian cryptographers for the army in Washington, starting on January 1, 1921. For Friedman the six-month contract was to be extended to a total of thirty-four years. Elizabeth was to serve a variety of government departments for almost as long and with only a few breaks.

Even when the contracts had been signed the Friedmans feared that some last-minute appeal by Fabyan might induce them, against their better judgment, to stay on at Riverbank. Evasive measures therefore had to be taken. First they sent for storage in Washington the possessions they had collected in their three-and-a-half years of married life. Then they quietly began to tie up the loose ends of their work at Riverbank. Only on the day of their departure did they break the news to Fabyan, appearing in their traveling clothes and explaining that they would be leaving that morning. A realist in practical matters, he accepted the situation with disgruntled good grace.

Chapter Five

The Move to Washington

W HEN THE FRIEDMANS began work in Washington for the army, the cryptographic establishment was settling down after a drastic reorganization. The United States had only reluctantly accepted the wartime necessity for cable vetting, the radio interception which had come with the development of wireless, and the acknowledgment of Bacon's dictum that "knowledge is power" however the knowledge is gained. Peace had thus brought the country to an ethical parting of the ways that it had never before approached. Did a nation continue to read, and to decipher if possible, the messages of foreign powers and private individuals, or did it return to prewar practice? Herbert Yardley, head of the Cipher Bureau whose fate was in the balance, was in no doubt; neither, he claimed, was informed opinion in Washington. "There was," he later wrote, "determination on every hand to continue the bureau during peace-time, for officials in all the departments recognised that in no other manner could the United States obtain an intimate knowledge of the true sentiments and intentions of other nations. They recognised that all the Great Powers maintained Cipher Bureaus, and that if the United States was to be placed on an equal footing it would be necessary to finance a group of skilled cryptographers."

After a good deal of heart searching, it was decided to demobilize the Shorthand Sub-Section of the Cipher Bureau and the Secret Ink Sub-Section, transfer the Code Compilation Sub-Section to the Signal Corps and restore Military Intelligence Communications to the Adjutant General of the army. This left only the Code and Cipher Solution Section: the Black Chamber as it became known, the organization which Friedman and his wife had been asked to join in 1919 and the organization whose operations, ostensibly ended in 1930, were then transferred with certain changes to Friedman himself.

Yardley estimated that 100,000 dollars a year would be needed to run the new interception and deciphering service. He succeeded in getting 40,000 of them from the State Department and the rest from Congress after taking some of their leaders into his confidence. As voted, the State Department money could not be legally spent within the District of Columbia — i.e., in Washington — and Yardley set up shop in a four-story brownstone house a few steps from New York's Fifth Avenue. "Practically all contact with the Government was now broken," he later wrote. "All the employees, including myself, were now civilians on secret pay-roll. The rent, telephone, lights, heat, office supplies — everything was paid for secretly so that no connection could be traced to the Government."

The British, whose cryptographic liaison with the Americans had virtually ceased with the end of the war, were more sophisticated. Many of the methods used by Room 40 during the war became illegal with the lapse of wartime regulations during 1919 and by the end of the year the exercise of the cryptographer's art had thus become circumscribed. However, a convenient method of restoring the situation was at hand.

Throughout 1919 the threat of insurrection in Ireland had constantly grown more serious. Something like a state of undeclared war existed and it was felt by the British Government that the Official Secrets Act of 1911, effective during the war only because strengthened by the now lapsed special regulations, was in need of reinforcement. The outcome was the Official Secrets Act, 1920, an act whose main sections dealt with the wearing of official uniforms, the forging of passports and the holding of official documents. There was some opposition in Parliament on the ground that the freedom of the press was threatened, but none at all to Section 4, which gave a secretary of state fresh and important powers. These enabled him, by issuing a warrant, to "require any person who owns or controls any telegraphic cable or wire, or any apparatus for wireless telegraphy, used for the sending or receipt of telegrams to or from any place out of the United Kingdom, to produce to him, or to any person named in the warrant, the originals and transcripts, either of all telegrams, or of telegrams of any specified class or description, or of telegrams sent from or addressed to any specified person or place sent or received to or from any place out of the United Kingdom by means of any such cable, wire, or apparatus, and all other papers relating to any such telegram as aforesaid."

On the face of it, the need for a Secretary of State to issue a warrant suggested that the reading of other people's mail, which could be ordered only when it was "in the public interest," would be a rare event. However, that does not seem to have been the case. Testifying before a U.S. Senate Committee in 1921, Clarence H.

Mackay, president of the Postal Telegraph Cable Company, stated: "Since censorship ceased the British Government have required us to turn over all messages ten days after they have been sent or received. This is a right which they claim under the landing licences they issue to all cable companies." Newcomb Carlton, president of the Western Union Telegraph Companies, gave details but went on to say that none of the messages were actually handled by Naval Intelligence and that their contents were therefore unknown to the British Government, a statement which may have been due either to ingenuousness or to the re-allocation of responsibility which had recently taken place in Britain. More than half a century later, in September, 1976, the company secretary of Western Union, commenting on evidence released by a U.S. Congressional Committee, is reported to have said: "It is the practice of the United Kingdom Government to pick up cable traffic from all carriers."

In the early 1920s preparations were going ahead for the rebirth of Room 40, killed off shortly after the end of the war. It soon reappeared as a section of the Foreign Office, staffed by such former members of the naval cryptographic team as Alastair Denniston and Joshua Cooper. Its work was unwittingly revealed in the House of Commons in 1927 by the foreign secretary, Sir Austen Chamberlain, after messages between Moscow and Russian officials in London had led to the rupture of Anglo-Russian trade relations. Sir Austen, refuting a denial that one particular message had been sent, commented: "M. Rosengolz may deny it. I think his denial was confined to the statement that no such telegram had been sent 'en clair' " — a virtual admission that the incriminating message had been sent in cipher, intercepted, and then deciphered.

The revival of secret cryptographic organizations in America and Britain was in both countries kept at least theoretically distinct from the other bodies which compiled codes and ciphers for the forces and at the same time tried to discover what potential enemies were compiling on the other side of the hill. It was the latter work

83

on which the Friedmans were first engaged in 1921. Many of the crypto-systems used in the war were no longer considered secure and for some months both Friedman and his wife toiled away at the comparatively routine business of developing low-level codes for the army.

Their first personal problem had been the prosaic one of trying to find a home. "We had arrived the last week in December, 1920, and I bought every issue of every newspaper as it came on the streets," Elizebeth Friedman remembers. "Yet the first unfurnished apartment was advertised exactly one year after the day of our arrival." Until then they lived in a music teacher's studio, a home that consisted of one small bedroom, a kitchen, a dinette, and a living room that faced Connecticut Avenue, with a long window-seat running across one wall, one grand piano, one upright piano, but virtually no other furniture.

"We had a wonderful life there for a year," she recalls. "We formed a music group. General Mauborgne — as he was to become — played the violin as did William Friedman. I played the piano, a friend we had known in Geneva, Illinois, played the cello, and a friend in the Army played the fourth instrument in the quartet. When the windows were open in the summer we used to have crowds listening in the street below."

It was a good life, very different from what they had known at Riverbank. "Our present environment," Friedman wrote in February to Dr. Manly, a former colleague and by this time Herbert Yardley's second-in-command of the Black Chamber, "is much more conducive to a normal, healthy, happy existence in this hard, cruel world, as they say. We find the work very interesting, and useful, and with a more cheerful prospect in view for the future. The rust of five years' hibernation has not yet begun to peel off, and it will take time. Mrs. Friedman calls upon me every now and then to be witness to the unmistakeable improvement in her disposition. And I am forced to admit that it was I who made her run the risk of an utterly ruined disposition! I fear that she is a bit more world-ly-wise than I am — or should I say now, *Was?* The Colonel hated her most fervently because she saw through him and his wiles very early in the game."

Yet it was not only Fabyan but the provincial atmosphere of Geneva that Friedman was glad to leave behind. "I can vouch for the authenticity of the picture of the typical American small town in the Middle West, as drawn by Lewis," he wrote to Manly when he had finished reading Sinclair Lewis's recently published *Main Street.* "I am glad I got away before I turned myself completely to brick-red iron ore dust. I'm afraid I haven't the pioneer spirit in me strong enough to buck that sort of thing, and maintain my equilibrium."

For Elizebeth Friedman, as well, Washington was a stimulating contrast to what she had known. "There were four legitimate theatres and I, who had grown up in rural Indiana, was starved for theatre," she has said. "We went at least three times a week." Even the weather persuaded them that with the move to Washington they were passing on to better things. The winter was beautiful, the days sunny, with no ice and very little snow, both of which had plagued them at Riverbank.

As winter turned to spring and spring to summer, as their con-tracts were renewed for a further six months and it became clear that Washington regarded them as indispensable, they grew even more confident. "Everything is fine down here," Friedman wrote to Dr. Eisenhour, the physicist in charge of Riverbank's experi-ments in acoustics. "Like the work and the people very much; a great deal more to live for, and many more friends and things to do. And freedom! Towards the last out there in Geneva it would not have taken much persuasion to have shuffled off, but it's all over now and I have put on lots of weight and feel fine. Much tennis, swimming and general out-doors."

He should have been satisfied. Few men have been more happily married and few have been better dovetailed into professional work which satisfied their special abilities. Yet beneath the pride in his growing reputation, beneath the outgoing social exterior of the man who enjoyed his tennis parties, the man welcomed everywhere, there flowed a persistent current of dissatisfaction. Deepest of all there was the subconscious worry of the immigrant making the best of a new world but an immigrant nevertheless. With Friedman there was also a regret which lingered throughout his life, the vestigial regret that he had forsaken genetics and biology for cryptography. However great an expert he knew himself to be within that particular discipline, however surely he was reestablishing cryptography on a scientific basis, he was beginning to learn how even in peacetime it became linked with events "about which," as he once commented, "the less said the better."

To this uncomfortable knowledge there were added two factors which combined to make life less than perfect. One was the intellectual climate of Washington in the early 1920s, by no means anti-Semitic but still preserving in Friedman's opinion, and in spite of all outward signs to the contrary, a division that did not have to be spoken, a division between them and us that cut an emigrant from Kishinev more deeply than most men.

And in Washington, as in London and Paris and Berlin, where the services were only slowly admitting that the arts of war could be strengthened by science, there stretched a gulf between the military tradition of obedience and the scientific tradition of questioning everything. Friedman's position was less invidious than that of the radio men and the physicists who a decade later fought for the acceptance of radar and the atomic bomb as weapons of war. His service in 1918 helped, and so did the fact that cryptography had a place, if not a specially honored one, in the military hierarchy. Nevertheless, throughout the interwar years, the Signal Corps in general and its cryptologists in particular were starved of men, money and equipment. Friedman not only knew it; a continuing splatter of comments in his private papers shows that he felt it, and often as a personal slight.

Nevertheless, the counterbalancing compensations were many. He was now recognized for what he was, a unique, one-off character who was master of his craft. At Riverbank he had been the personal employee, if not the personal servant, of Colonel Fabyan. In the army both his position and his ambition had been circumscribed by service regulations. Here he was civilian cryptologist — *the* cryptologist — Office of the Chief Signal Officer, Washington, D.C.

This position was confirmed at the end of 1921 when he became, officially, Chief Cryptanalyst to the War Department, a post which he was to occupy for a quarter of a century before becoming director of Communications Research in the newly formed Army Security Agency. At the changeover, in 1947, it was found that although he had from the summer of 1922 been in the Army Reserve he had not, since demobilization in 1919, been a member of the National Army. He had not been fully vetted. And it was then discovered, to the embarrassment of the authorities, that the man who had led the only wartime enterprise as secret and as sensitive as manufacture of the first nuclear weapons, had never been given full security clearance.

By 1922 Friedman's position in the cryptographic establishment was assured and in 1929 a drastic reorganization of America's cryptographic and intelligence services was to give it considerably greater importance. During the years between, he was steadily transformed from a purely official expert for the army into the man automatically consulted in Washington about any cryptographic problem, whatever its source.

Early in 1922 the Friedmans moved into another furnished apartment; then, in the summer of 1923, into a handsome rambling house in five acres of grounds in Maryland. Seventy-foot tulip magnolia trees surrounded it, open country stretched away from it, no other building could be seen from it, and they named it "Green Mansions" after W. H. Hudson's novel. For the first time in their lives Friedman and his wife could devote themselves to building up what they hoped would be a permanent home of their own, and here their daughter Barbara was born.

"During our two years residence at Green Mansions," Mrs. Friedman has written, "we learned that anyone who has a country place or a watering place never becomes lonely; indeed, one hardly has an opportunity to do what one wishes, or even one's chores on the place because everyone who needs entertainment, or wants to pass the time at week-ends and summer evenings, invariably drops in. Each year at Green Mansions we must have entertained more people to outdoor parties than we would have done at a town house." This was much to her husband's liking. An almost alarming ability to concentrate on his work was matched with a taste for social life, and during these early years in Washington it successfully helped him bear the mental strain of an occupation whose complexities, technical and ethical, were even then beginning to grow. However, as work accumulated and hours lengthened Friedman found himself oppressed by the two-hour drive into the center of Washington each morning and the drive out through the evening rush. Eventually Green Mansions was given up for the comfortable Chevy Chase house that was to be home for a quarter of a century, and where their son John Ramsay Friedman was born in 1926.

Although most of his work was done in the Munitions Building, it overflowed into his spare time at home — "he could not tolerate not being busy every minute," his wife once said — and here he wrote *Elements of Cryptanalysis,* a manual which brought order into the chaos of contemporary crytographic exposition, and which he later expanded into the four-volume *Elements of Cryptanalysis* which became the U.S. Army's cryptographic Bible.

In the larger work Friedman gave an illustration of what even his best friends sometimes called luck and which he believed was intuition. A 443-letter cryptogram had been submitted to the War Department for solution and after some preliminary work he decided to concentrate on the beginning of the sentence, for which he already had letters and blanks running as follows: * * T T H * * * * . The message, Friedman said with confidence, must start with the two words "But though." So they did, although the chances of any message starting with these two words were minute.

Many of his writings had not only orderly exposition but also style. A paper on "The Principles of Indirect Symmetry of Position in Secondary Alphabets and Their Application in the Solution of Polyalphabetic Substitution Ciphers" might not appear to offer much nontechnical enjoyment. But in explaining what happened to fifty test messages submitted by a Mr. Burdick who expected them to be insoluble, he comments: "By superimposing the messages the writer solved them and completely reconstructed both basic alphabets, *by applying and extending the principles of indirect symmetry of position that were first discovered by Mr. Burdick himself!* It is not often that a cryptanalyst unknowingly discovers the very weapon that deals the death-blow to his own brain-child!"

Friedman lectured regularly on "The Solution of Military Codes and Ciphers" to officers at the Signal Corps School at Camp Vail, and took part in maneuvers during which he supervised the use of the new codes and cipher systems whose compilation was a routine part of his work. However, he did not tackle these compilations in a routine way for long. "You recall your jocular reference, in your Biliteral talk, to the fact that 'Friedman is damn lazy,' " he wrote to Fabyan. "Well, possibly laziness of the same nature had something to do with it, but at any rate I recently devised a method of preparing codes which will, if I am to judge by the enthusiastic reception accorded to the system by those higher up, revolutionise methods of compilation. A demonstration is to be given very shortly before high officials. I estimate that it will reduce the amount of work involved in the present methods by over 75%."

Relaxing with his wife on a canoe trip up the Potomac River, 1921.

Green Mansions, the Friedman home from 1923 to 1925.

*Mrs. Elizebeth Friedman, 1928, with her daughter Barbara,
aged five, and her son John Ramsay, aged two.*

In view of all that had happened, and despite constant bickerings, Friedman's relations with Colonel Fabyan continued to rub along on this not too unfriendly basis. At first this seems strange. Yet the attitudes of both men, some of the reasons for their constant disagreements, and a hint of how they managed to carry on, are all contained in a letter from Fabyan written after he had balked at printing a paper by Friedman. "I can sympathise with you in your desires to plant your name in the Halls of Fame," he wrote, "but I don't want to obligate myself to do anything which may not fit into my game at a certain time. On the other hand, it might suit my purpose to ask for your picture, a short biography, and a foreword, signed by you, in publishing the work on cipher and codes, but I am not going to obligate myself to publish anything in any manner. I am not in the publishing business. If I cannot have your work without restrictions, I will have to do without it. You are certainly entitled to the privileges of the seller and I claim the privileges of the buyer. . . ."

Shortly afterwards Fabyan asked if Friedman would do a job of decipherment for him and send in the bill. Friedman, duly cautious, asked for a fee of 150 dollars, to be paid in advance. Fabyan offered 50 dollars. Friedman, believing that the result would be published only under the Riverbank imprint, and that the fee offered was in any case derisory, then offered to do the job for nothing — but only on the legal agreement that his name would be printed as author. The offer does not seem to have been taken up.

Despite their differences, the two men remained in contact, and the colonel frequently asked his former employee for advice on the most bizarre of problems. There was, for example, his own view of how the old A.T.&T. problem could be handled. "In my opinion," he wrote, "the most successful printing machine telegraph will handle the message by a ray of light projected on a film, making an undulating wave which, on being fed through the machine, will be translated by vibrations into a horn audible to the ear. This, in

William Friedman with the Hebern cipher machine, the first in the United States to utilize rotors.

my opinion, will be difficult of decipherment in as much as the wave varies with the pitch and timbre of a person's voice; giving two films bearing the same message of a very different appearance." There is no record of a reply.

Friedman's alleged luck, illustrated by the 443-letter cryptogram submitted to the War Department, produced the saying that he was like Midas but that in his case "everything he touched turned to plain-text." In such a view there is almost certainly an over-emphasis on luck in contrast with intuition. Yet in two ways he was lucky: he had come on the cryptographic scene just when war and the development of wireless were together multiplying the demand for cryptographers; and he had since his youth had a rough-and-ready knowledge of electricity and engineering and had always hankered after more. "I wish I had a thorough technical training in fundamental physics and electricity," he once wrote to Fabyan. "I get ideas about the subject but don't know enough about the subject to work them out."

This was an unusual interest for a cryptographer and was invaluable in the 1920s and 1930s when electromechanical enciphering systems came into being. As early as 1915 a Californian, Edward H. Hebern, had designed an enciphering device in which two electric typewriters were joined by twenty-six wires randomly connected, so that a plaintext letter tapped out on one machine would automatically produce an enciphered letter on the second. Six years later, on March 31, 1921, Hebern filed a patent for an enciphering machine incorporating what he called an "electric code." This was a "rotor," a unit which was to become, in one of many forms, an essential of a whole generation of enciphering machines.

The value of the rotor is easy to understand. It consists of a disc on each face of which there are a number of electrical contacts. The contacts usually number twenty-six on each face, and are arranged around the circumferences so that each contact on one face connects at random to a contact on the other face. The impulse from a plaintext letter typed on an electrical machine will enter through one of the contacts and will emerge through a contact on the other face to produce a different, and thus enciphered, letter on a second typewriter. However, any movement of the rotor from one position to another will produce a different encipherment. Thus a rotor with the normal twenty-six available contacts can produce twenty-six cipher alphabets. Nor is this all. If a second rotor is added to the machine, and so geared that it starts to move forward one contact at a time whenever the first rotor has completed a revolution, then the number of possibilities will be 26 by 26, or 676. The addition of each fresh rotor will multiply the possibilities by twenty-six, so that a five-rotor machine will offer the staggering number of between 11 and 12 million possible alphabets.

By 1924 Hebern had interested the U.S. Navy in his machine and had built a five-rotor model which was tested at the Navy Building in Washington. At first something inexplicable appeared to be wrong since there were constant electrical problems; fuses blew and solenoids burned out. The director of Naval Communications then ordered that tests be made at his home, and here no troubles developed, although back at the Navy Building the same problems were repeated. It was some time later that the experts discovered what was wrong: the Navy Building was still on direct current while the director's home had been turned over to alternating current.

Eventually the navy ordered two of Hebern's latest machines, with a promise to buy many more if the ciphers produced were as safe in operation as they appeared to be. At this point, Lieutenant Strubel, the head of the navy's Code and Signal Section in the Office of Naval Communications, called in Friedman. Neither of the two navy machines could be spared so Friedman ordered two for the army. "The rotor wirings of the Army's machines were altogether different from those of the Navy, a fact which I discovered simply by asking Strubel to encipher a few letters on his machine, using settings I specified," Friedman subsequently said. "After some study I reported that in my opinion the security of the machine was not as great as Navy thought. The result was a challenge which I accepted."

The navy provided ten messages, a contrast with the hundreds of messages a day which would probably be available when the machine was in use. Each message, moreover, consisted of only about two dozen letters. "He told me many times," Mrs. Friedman said later, "that he sat before those messages for about six weeks, becoming discouraged almost to the point of break-down, before he even thought of a method of tackling them. Then he did tackle them, then he did solve them."

Friedman did so by putting the letters in the messages on strips of paper, then sliding them back and forth until some phenomenon arose in one column, then another phenomenon in another. "The index of coincidence," and Friedman's intuition, did the rest and provided the answer.

The solution of the ten navy messages, the first solution in history of a wired-rotor cipher machine, did not entirely kill Hebern's prospects. His machine was adapted, and some of the new models were put into use. Eventually, however, in Friedman's words, the "Navy dropped negotiations with Hebern when it became obvious that he was not competent to build what the Navy wanted and needed."

The Hebern machine quite fortuitously provided Friedman with a good example of how dangerous it was to send any cipher message in actual word-lengths instead of in groups of the same length. One man, anxious to obtain a permanent post in the Signal Service, claimed to Friedman that he had deciphered a test message enciphered on one of Hebern's machines sold for commercial use, and had found it to be some lines of poetry. This it no doubt was, but Friedman remained convinced that it could not have been deciphered by normal methods. How, then, could the result have been

obtained? There was, it appeared, only one way. The searcher had
followed a hunch that this particular message was poetry and had
then plodded through many pages of likely originals until he found
a passage whose word lengths exactly matched the word lengths
of the encoded message. Faced with the deception the man admitted what he had done.

The message had not been "deciphered" in the proper sense of
the word and would have remained undeciphered had, as an example, " 'Twas back in the summer of seventy five" been rewritten,
before encipherment, as: TWA SBA CKI INT HES UMM ERO FSE VEN
TYF IVE. Instead, the enciphered message had been printed as:

KB BTR EKSMO DG TNS GDNX AAT XCN ICA IDUSEA
AJEF HI RGZ TKCD FP AQWDJ YD MON ZK DA JGE
ONW HXTCHQC WOSG WTMCP BN RF GUUKHEJ II XHR
WARRVH FQ QIKCW HGBQLY PWVHYROT SMHLME
PHGEEPNFY.

The man who received the message, instinctively feeling it to be
poetry, eventually found: "In the photo of her hero / She can see
/ Things that do not show so clear to / You or Me / For her
outlook ever seems / To be colored by her dreams / In which
golden sunshine gleams / Endlessly."

Investigation of the Hebern machine was an early example of
Friedman's cooperation with the navy, which flourished increasingly after he struck up a friendship with Captain, later Admiral,
Wenger that was to last for the rest of their lives. However, it was
not only service work of the expected kind that kept him occupied.
The Carnegie Institution, Washington, D.C., required the decoding of messages sent in the eighteenth century from the British
minister in Philadelphia to the governor of Nova Scotia and, almost inevitably, Friedman was conscripted for the job. When the
planet Mars came close to the earth, the Signal Corps alerted three

97

radio stations to listen for possible signals and at least some messages were recorded on Ediphone cylinders. "They came in on 21,000 metres," Friedman was told. "They consisted in part of dashes of six second duration, separated by intervals of six seconds. These dashes continued for several minutes and were followed by a voice pronouncing words. They were isolated words of from one to four syllables. Evidently this was a test of some sort, but we have been unable so far to discover who was doing the testing and we can't understand the words." Perhaps Friedman, it was suggested, would be interested in listening. No messages were discovered.

He was also brought into the Teapot Dome scandal of 1924 which centered on the sale of government property — including the Teapot Dome site — for use by private developers. It ended in a long prison sentence for the U.S. Secretary of the Interior, Albert Fall, the resignation or expulsion of two other members of the cabinet, and the self-exile of some of the minor characters who fled from the United States to escape prosecution. An important element in the convictions was the decoding of messages sent by Edward Beale McLean, the publisher of the *Washington Post*. McLean was not himself involved in the scandal but seemed to have been used as a go-between for the industrialist Edward Doheny and the secretary of the interior. Friedman gave the crucial evidence in the Senate hearings which eventually led to the trial and as a result received nationwide publicity for what was lauded as a remarkable feat.

He himself knew better, and subsequently put the facts down in a private memorandum. "The decoding of those messages was certainly no remarkable feat, nor was it even one calling for any skill beyond the ability of the average code clerk," he declared. "For as a matter of fact, the translation of the particular messages to which so much publicity was given [those passing between Mr. E. B. McLean and his agents] was not accomplished by 'breaking down' the messages, or by a cryptanalytical process, as it is designated scientifically, but merely by reference to the proper code book. In other words, the despatches were not 'broken' — they were merely 'read.' "

Yet the story that he tells is in many ways a remarkable one. It began on February 28 when the text of several telegrams, entered into evidence the previous day, was released for publication in the press. Reading them in the newspapers that evening, Friedman immediately saw that they were not cipher messages but code messages, written with the help of a code-book. There were only four of them; all were short and it would be almost impossible to discover what they meant without access to the code-book. "A cryptanalyst with a very highly developed sense of imagination, and with many extraneous clues to guide him might, if given sufficient time, arrive at a probable reading of a few of the code groups," Friedman wrote, "but such a reading would rest upon entirely undemonstrable hypotheses, and it would bear absolutely no weight with any critical group of laymen, not to speak of its being considered as trustworthy evidence by an unbiased jury."

The following morning he was approached by a journalist from one of the press agencies. Would Friedman attempt to decode the messages for the service? But Friedman, on the staff of one official agency, felt it would be improper for him to dabble, unofficially, in the affairs of another. However, later in the day Senator Walsh of Montana, the committee "prosecutor," asked for his aid. The chief signal officer gave permission, and Friedman spent the next five hours in his own office and in the Library of Congress, searching among a large collection of commercial and private code-books to find the right one. He had no luck.

The next day, however, the *New York World* published plaintext versions of the messages, together with the statement that they had been written with the help of a code used by agents of the Department of Justice. To Friedman, who knew that the mere knowledge of what code-book had been used would not help in the solution

99

of messages, one thing was obvious: the paper had somehow gained access to the code-book. He now called upon the Department of Justice, borrowed a copy of the code, and discovered that, substantially, the messages read as reported by the *World*.

Friedman's formal testimony, given shortly afterwards, brought him a public fame he did not relish. His discomfiture was natural: the more sensational claims made included the statement that he had earlier "discovered the Bi-literal Cipher in Shakespeare's Works, disclosing that Bacon was a Son of Queen Elizabeth."

One unexpected result of the Teapot Dome case was a call from McLean. His friendship with many of those involved made him feel that in future it would be unwise to use ordinary means of communication. Would Friedman, he asked, construct a secure two-part private code for his personal use? A contract was drawn up and the Friedmans spent the winter of 1924 on the job. William Friedman directed the enterprise and took charge when he got back home in the evenings while his wife did the hour-by-hour work of compiling the code during the day.

A request of a different kind came from a different quarter in 1925. Walter Arensberg, a millionaire graduate from Harvard, and later one of America's most persistent patrons of the arts, was both a student of Italian and an amateur cryptographer. It was not surprising, as Friedman once wrote, that "he should select Dante as his first victim." Having claimed in *The Cryptography of Dante* that the Italian had embedded scores of hidden messages in his words, Arensberg turned to Shakespeare. *The Cryptography of Shakespeare,* privately published in 1922, was planned to be the first of two volumes, but the second was slow in coming and Friedman was approached. Would he, Arensberg asked, take a full-time post aimed at proving the Baconian authorship of Shakespeare?

Friedman refused, first pleading the importance of his official work and then continuing: "At the same time my experience with modern cryptography and cryptanalysis leads me to view the details and methods of attempts to prove the case for Bacon with the critical eye of a cold-blooded scientist, who employs his imaginative faculty only to advance hypotheses, forces it to stop right there, and uses none of it in the demonstration of the proof or falsity of the hypotheses so erected. I am sorry to say that I did not find that this was the attitude of Mrs. Gallup and her associates, and, so far as I am concerned, the validity of her work is very much open to question. . . ."

By this time it was not only Friedman himself who was being sought after for freelance cryptological assignments. When he was unavailable, it was often his wife who was second on the list. In fact one of the legends which grew up around the Friedmans was that it was she who had taught him the fundamentals of the craft. If any teaching was to be done it was certainly by him; nevertheless, it is true that Elizebeth Friedman had much the same facility as her husband for seeing through the letters of an enciphered message towards the essentials of the plaintext that lay underneath. After the year's work for the army she had resigned to put Green Mansions in order and in the hope of writing a book. Only a few months later the Navy Department, having failed to lure Friedman away from the Munitions Building, turned to his wife and for almost a year she worked on a part-time basis for the department's code-compilation department.

Something more important was on the way, however. By the early 1920s the U.S. Coast Guard Service, a law enforcement agency of the Treasury, was doing its best to cope with the huge increase in liquor smuggling which had followed the start of the Prohibition era in 1920. In the early days most of the cargoes had been run into the New York area, but by 1925 the more popular routes had become those between Florida and the Bahamas, and Florida and Cuba. The liquor smugglers were highly organized, made frequent use of enciphered or encoded messages, and presented the authorities with a threat that could only be removed by a counter-intelligence campaign. A cryptologist was badly needed and the Coast Guard, like the navy, having failed to recruit Friedman, approached his wife.

"I was called on by Captain Charles Root, a Coast Guard officer who had the title of Intelligence Officer," she says, "and I was soon afterwards appointed as a 'special agent' to be paid by the Department of Justice, on loan to Captain Root. A special agent in those days was someone who did not have to conform to the requirements of office hours but is expected to go wherever, and be wherever, he can best pursue the investigation on which he is engaged. Thus it came about that I was able to do the work at home for which I was requested. I went to Captain Root's office, collected papers and information, took them home, and returned them when the work had been done."

She was soon given what she later looked back on as a salutary lesson. A single long message had arrived in the United States by telegraph from Havana and almost certainly had some connection with liquor running. It was quickly seen to have been written in a transposition cipher; and, since there was but one message available it could only be solved, if at all, by a lengthy process of trial and error. However, the problem would be immensely simplified if the key word were known. A very young lieutenant in the Coast Guard suggested that this might be "Havana." "I laughed at him," Mrs. Friedman remembers, "saying that no-one in his right mind would ever use as a keyword the name of the city from which he was sending a message." However, after laboriously working through scores of possibilities, she tried "Havana" as a last resort. It was the word. "I decided," she says, "that I would never again allow my mind to become so rigid as to exclude the obvious."

The work for the Coast Guard increased. Elizebeth Friedman began to appear in court as an expert witness and was soon visiting the West Coast to give onshore Coast Guardsmen courses in simple cryptography. Eventually the Treasury Department decided to set up a full-time cryptologic unit and she was given the task of running it. While the unit was to have its headquarters in the Coast Guard it was to serve all five of the law enforcement bureaus of the Treasury Department and have a small staff of men with qualifications in mathematics, physics or chemistry. They, it was hoped, would provide the cryptologists of the future.

As head of the unit, Elizebeth Friedman was starting two decades' cryptologic work for the government that steadily grew in importance with the approach of the Second World War. In 1941 the entire unit was put under control of the navy, but before this she played a key part in many sensational cases. One dealt with two brothers, well known to the authorities and believed by the Treasury to be among the most efficient of San Francisco's dope runners. No hard evidence was available until one of their letters was intercepted. It had been posted in Shanghai, but contained only a long string of what appeared to be gibberish, dotted with such "words" as "wyvas," "wyrras" and "wysats." The text was radioed to Mrs. Friedman who quickly saw that the message used a double-code system. It was soon broken, to reveal a message reading: "Our shipment goes today. It consists of 520 tins of smoking opium and 20 tins sample, 70 oz. cocaine, 70 oz. morphine, 40 oz. heroin. . . ."

This was good, but not yet good enough. Then, a few days later, a second message in the same code was intercepted, passed on, and found to contain the necessary evidence: the brothers were to look for the narcotics in eight numbered drums of tung oil due to arrive shortly in the Japanese merchant ship *Asama Maru*. The contraband was discovered, the brothers pleaded guilty, and each was given the maximum sentence of twelve years. That would give them time, one newspaper commented, to work out a code that couldn't be broken by a woman.

In this case the physical evidence was enough to secure conviction and Mrs. Friedman was not called. The following year she not only gave evidence in one of the more colorful liquor-running cases but conducted what an enthusiastic press described as "a courtroom class in Cryptography." This was held after Mrs. Friedman gave evidence of deciphering many key messages used in the prosecution's case. The whole basis of cryptography then came under attack as one of the defense lawyers, Edwin H. Grace, claimed that the cipher word alleged to mean "alcohol" might just as easily mean "bananas" or "coconuts." Mrs. Friedman demonstrated that when a cipher system has been worked out no doubt can be entertained about any particular word. But the defense was unwilling to give in. She then turned to the judge and asked: "Your Honor, is there a blackboard available to the Court?" A blackboard was brought in and on it she wrote the name of one of the liquors involved, THE OLD COLONEL. She then pointed out that the words contained three "l"s and three "o"s. Next, she wrote on the board, below the letters of THE OLD COLONEL, their cipher equivalents.

She now scanned the material she had used as evidence and found a number of other words containing the letters "l" and "o." In each case the cipher equivalents were the same and the defense decided not to press their point. Amos Woodcock, the chief prosecution lawyer, writing later to the secretary of the treasury, commented of the messages that "without their translations, I do not believe that this very important case would have been won."

By far the best known of the many cases in which Elizebeth Friedman's Treasury unit provided vital evidence was that of the *I'm Alone,* a small vessel ostensibly under Canadian registry and carrying liquor from Belize, British Honduras, to the Gulf of Mexico where her cargo was transferred to small boats. Sighted by the U.S. Coast Guard within the three-mile limit, the ship hove anchor and fled to sea. Followed and ordered to stop for searching, she refused to do so and was then sunk by a single shot from the U.S.

Coast Guard vessel, whose captain had intended merely to fire across her bows.

The Canadian Government lost no time in filing a damage suit against the United States for $250,000. This was countered by the Americans on the grounds that the vessel had not been owned by Canadians at all but by Americans. Defense was difficult and might have been impossible but for the intervention of Elizebeth Friedman. Working in Houston, Texas, on a trunkload of code and cipher messages all involved in rum-running cases, she suddenly realized that one series of messages stood out from the others. They had passed between British Honduras and various cable addresses in New York City, and a rapid check showed that the quantities of smuggled liquor recorded were similar to those on the Belize manifests which gave the successive loadings of the *I'm Alone*.

It was but the start of a long trail which eventually led to a well-known rumrunner on the Atlantic coast with at least one conviction to his name. He was arrested, but only after the murder of one witness who had turned state's evidence. Mrs. Friedman gave evidence in the Washington arbitration case which ended the *I'm Alone* case; it was not until some time later that she discovered she had been specially guarded following threats of an attempt on her life.

Friedman himself sometimes helped the Coast Guard when on leave from his official work with the army, and once spent a fortnight at sea on one of the special Coast Guard cutters intercepting rumrunners' radio messages. He deciphered a number on the spot, and gave a brief instruction course to those who would be doing the work in future. Back on shore, he ruminated on the fact that the opposition would, once they realized their codes and ciphers were being broken, try to get one step ahead again.

"Here's what I predict," he wrote to the captain of the cutter he had sailed in. "Within half a year, if your programme goes through, you will find the [rumrunners] using motorised mobile radio transmitter stations for their shore equipment. They will stay in one position only long enough to set up and transmit the traffic. Then they will roll away, and on the next schedule they will be somewhere else. They are smart enough to see that with efficient compass-work on the Commanding General's part they can't hope to operate a fixed shore station for more than a day or two, and since their experience is absolutely conclusive in its teaching, viz. that a paralyzed shore station paralyzes all activity, the next step, mobile transmitters, will be apparent to them within a short time."

Friedman himself never gave evidence in court in a liquor-running case and thus avoided the inevitable publicity, much to the satisfaction of the army. But his wife's work unfailingly made news, whatever steps she took to minimize it, and the repercussions sometimes brought protests. Such was the case with "Key Woman of the T-Men," an article published only after the author had cleared it with both the Treasury and the Public Relations Department of the army. Despite this, Friedman was soon afterwards visited by the Inspector General of the army and asked to explain why his name had been mentioned in the article.

There were, however, specific occasions which did genuinely demand secrecy: those which revealed that the Treasury unit was deciphering messages not only in English but also in Oriental languages. "To practically everyone, 'Oriental languages' means Japanese and Chinese," Elizabeth wrote in one memorandum to the commandant of the Coast Guard. "In view of the present situation in the Far East, I know definitely that to mention that we have ever solved a message in Japanese or Chinese will bring down upon the Coast Guard, the certain anathema of the Navy Department, and possibly of the State and War departments."

Her work was interrupted when, in 1928, she became a minor member of the American delegation to the International Telegraph Conference in Brussels, a delegation to which Friedman himself acted as both executive secretary and technical adviser. His appointment typified the fact that he had now become in some ways a general duties adviser to the government. He had earlier written *The History of the Use of Code and Code Language,* a book published by the Government Printing Office in which the word code was used in its technical sense to describe the language medium employed to transmit by telegraph, radio and cable. Thus when the first international conference in the field of communications was held in Washington in October, 1927, it was not surprising that he should be picked as the Americans' technical adviser. He turned out to be an agreeable as well as a competent man for the job and the meeting had barely finished when he was snapped up to appoint and direct the staff for the next year's meeting in Brussels.

For both the Friedmans the autumn weeks in Brussels were an interminable round of committee meetings and larger conferences. There was little time for more than work and both hoped that when the conference was over they could squeeze in a little European travel. They succeeded, although rather unexpectedly.

Friedman had technically been on duty in Brussels for the State Department. Before the conference was finished, however, there came orders from the War Department, directing him north to Stockholm in order to meet Boris Hagelin, the man who was to provide the backbone of America's tactical crypto-systems during the Second World War, and who became the only known person to make a fortune from an activity restricted to the invention and design of ciphering machines.

The army's interest in Hagelin in 1926 sprang from the birth and development in Europe of more than one series of mechanical and electromechanical ciphering devices comparable to the Hebern machine in which alphabetic sequences could be mounted to produce constantly changing sequences of cipher alphabets. The first of these, made by the Cipher-Machine Company of Berlin in the 1920s and eventually incorporating the rotor principle as developed by the German Arthur Scherbius, was appropriately named Enigma.

The U.S. delegation to the International Telegraph Conference in Brussels, 1928. William Friedman, Secretary, standing fourth from right.

In the early models the electrical paths between the elements representing plaintext characters and those representing their cipher equivalents, shown on small lettered bulbs which lit up, were varied by means of a frame carrying insulated wires. This frame could be moved by means of a cam between two fixed contact-bearing members, one on each side of it, thus changing the electrical paths between the keyboard and the printing mechanism. The method was cumbersome and soon replaced by rotors.

From the first Friedman seems to have sensed that he should take special interest in the Enigma and as early as 1926 he had succeeded, apparently with the help of the U.S. military attaché at the Hague, in obtaining a detailed report on the machine from a cryptologist in the Dutch Army. "Considering the machine with reference to the security it offers against unauthorised deciphering, I must say that it satisfies all requirements, however high they may be," the report said. "Being an expert in ciphering and deciphering matters, I do not hesitate to say that even possession of a comparable machine with the same electrical connections, both in the ciphering cylinders and in the other parts of the machine, will not enable an unauthorised person, even though he is an expert, to decipher a particular document or to find its solution by means of scientific methods; unless, that is, he knows the complete key [that is, the order of the ciphering cylinders *and* the adjustment of the letter-rings *and* that of the letters appearing in the windows].

"Owing to the extraordinary length of the period of each key, as well as of the enormous number of different keys being possible, it may be said without any reservation that the security offered by 'Enigma' against any attempt at unauthorised deciphering is absolute."

Friedman managed to buy at least one Enigma machine in the late 1920s, and possibly two. He then spent considerable time trying to discover how messages enciphered with it could, despite the Dutch report, be deciphered without detailed knowledge of cylin-

William Friedman about 1928.

ders, letter rings, and letters. He had little success.

However, the rotor principle had been developed in Europe not only by Scherbius but also by the Dutchman Hugo Koch, and the Swede Arvid Gerhard Damm. Here was the link with Hagelin, since Damm's rotors were to be used on a commercial scale in a machine designed by Hagelin in 1925.

Born in 1892 in a small town not far from Baku, southern Russia, where his father was at that time the manager of the Nobel Brothers Oil Company's oilfields and refineries, Hagelin had first come into contact with Damm when, in 1921, Emanuel Nobel, the then head of the Nobel Oil Company and his father's closest friend, injected money into the enterprise, which was developing Damm's inventions but which had become bankrupt. Hagelin, Jr., was chosen to supervise this company. "A large number of different devices were designed and built under Damm's supervision over the years," Hagelin later said, "but very few came into practical use. Damm's tragedy was that he was a pioneer; he had to start from scratch with his machines; he did not have a designer's mind, and therefore had trouble in coming to practical solutions. What was still worse, the market for ciphering machines was then practically non-existent."

However, the situation was changing even before Damm died in 1927, and quite independently of the Enigma machine's success. The Swedish General Staff had in 1925 been considering the purchase of the Enigma machine and the young Hagelin decided to make a competitive entry with a machine based on Damm's rotors but considerably simplified, and similar in shape and operation to the German machine. This machine was later redesigned so that it could be operated in the same manner as an electric typewriter, producing the text printed on a tape.

There was thus good reason for Friedman to visit the Swedish works in 1927. He did not meet Hagelin himself on this occasion, but was able to learn a good deal before making a leisurely return home, stopping first in Copenhagen and then in London so that he and his wife could meet friends they had made at the Brussels conference.

His success there made William Friedman an obvious choice for the International Radio Conference in Madrid in 1932, a meeting which he attended in a double capacity: first as technical adviser and committee chairman to, and of, the U.S. delegation, and secondly, as the U.S. representative of the International Telegraph Conference. This time Mrs. Friedman, fully occupied with her antismuggling activities at the Treasury, was unable to travel with him when he left Washington in August.

The work, he was soon assuring her, was even more concentrated than it had been in Brussels. "Usually I go right back to the office (after dinner)," he wrote, "and begin sorting out the new documents which are coming in a perfect torrent. These, numerous enough in French, are translated and mimeographed by our staff, making an equally voluminous river of English translations to sort out. The sorting alone takes an hour. Not to say anything about looking over the contents, seeing what is of interest, filing the letter, etc."

By the end of September it was clear that the conference would continue for many more weeks, possibly months, and Friedman began urging his wife, first by letter, then by telephone, to join him. "Finally," she says, "I worked out a plan which would enable me to go. I made up my mind one Tuesday night and within two days had arranged affairs at my office and at my home, and arranged for my two children and housekeeper to stay with my sister in Detroit. I myself left New York on the *Isle de France* for Le Havre on the Friday, two and a half days after I had made up my mind."

The Friedmans remained in Madrid until late November. Then, when the army authorities ordered him to return despite the fact that the conference was continuing, they began to make for home via Seville and Granada, planning to sail from the port nearest to the Straits of Gibraltar. Before they reached it the army changed its mind, Friedman was recalled to the conference, and it was mid-December before they finally returned on the *Leviathan,* reaching Washington two days before Christmas.

Friedman's work as an official U.S. delegate in Brussels and Madrid reinforced his position in the cryptographic hierarchy. Between these two events, however, there had taken place a traumatic upheaval in America's code-and-cipher-breaking operations. But while this upheaval raised Friedman's professional standing it was also to increase the mental stresses which had been building up as he tried to resolve the problems of living a normal life within the security establishment.

In 1927 he had consulted Dr. Philip Graven, a young Washington psychoanalyst, and for six months saw him regularly to discuss psychiatric difficulties. Just what they were remains as uncertain today as it was half a century ago for Friedman had already become one of the unfortunate few who even in peacetime had to conceal some of their problems not only from wives but from psychiatrists. However, his subsequent history leaves little doubt that his problems included the strains of developing a double personality. The affable Friedman, always a desirable guest, always the adored father, always the normal sociable animal, seemed basically different from the other Friedman who had to think thrice before he spoke.

The strain was more than enough to account for the breakdowns which were to take place every few years. But between them Friedman was, says his daughter, "the attentive, witty and generous father who took my brother and me, and our friends and neighbourhood kids, on excursions to 'Indian Rock' for climbing and picnicing, to magic shows at the Old Belasco Theatre, to Rock Creek Park, and to family vacations at the seashore." But behind the happy exterior the problems remained. They were to be compounded early in the 1930s.

Since 1921 he had exercised his talents in areas which could usually be openly acknowledged even if they could not be described in detail. Codes and ciphers had to be compiled for the army's use in war, the federal authorities had to be helped in law enforcement, but if secrecy had to be maintained it was legitimate secrecy, maintained within the accepted conventions. The darker sides were ruled over by Herbert Yardley with his covert Black Chamber and its brief to discover, by any means possible, what encoded or enciphered messages were passing between foreign diplomats in the United States and their masters abroad.

Yardley's organization was administered by the officer in charge of the communications office in the army's military intelligence, at first Colonel Moorman, then Major Millikan, and from 1927 Lieutenant Colonel O. S. Albright. After little more than a year in charge, Colonel Albright decided that the Black Chamber should be transferred to the Signal Corps where training, as well as operations, could be carried on without difficulty. The Chief of Staff assented to the change in May, 1929, and soon afterwards preparations for the reorganization were begun. Meanwhile, however, Yardley approached the new secretary of state, Henry Stimson, brought into office following the election of Herbert Hoover a few months earlier. Wanting more money, Yardley with some pride presented Stimson with an outline of the Black Chamber's formidable achievements during the previous eight years. Stimson, who had not known that the organization existed, responded unexpectedly with the terse comment that "gentlemen do not read each other's mail," and the decision to withdraw the State Department's $40,000 a year, a move which he knew would effectively close down the Black Chamber.

Three months' pay in advance went to all members of the staff but for all practical purposes the organization ceased to exist in May, 1929. "This fine gesture," commented the *Christian Science Monitor* later, "will commend itself to all who are trying to develop the same standards of decency between Governments as exist between individuals. The practice is a left-over from the secret diplomacy which the World War was supposed to have overthrown. It has no place in a world which is working for peace based on trust and good will."

However, in spite of Stimson's honest intentions, the fine gesture did not go so very far in practice. This is revealed in extracts (in the William F. Friedman Collection, George C. Marshall Research Library, Lexington, Virginia) from "U.S. Army in World War II: The Signal Corps," a manuscript history prepared in the 1940s by the Office of the Chief of Military History, S.S.U.S.A. "Mr. Yardley," it says, "was left to assume that code-breaking had been discontinued altogether.

"It had not been. . . . The Military Intelligence Division which had subcontracted its cryptanalytic work to Yardley now transferred it to the Office of the Chief Signal Officer, and transferred the responsibility, too." The brief, the history goes on to comment, gave authority for solution of enemy messages in time of war only. "However," it continues, "it became apparent that an army could not begin reading the enemy's codes on the day a war began. One must learn before that event, though doing so meant violating the privacy of powers still officially friendly. This was the inescapable result of the general use of codes by nations, part of a universal trespass recognised quite apart from conventional standards of international morality." Gentlemen, in fact, went on reading other people's mail, although under a more plausible cover.

Friedman, moreover, was to be the civilian cryptologist in charge of a new organization, the Signal Intelligence Service, specially set up to combine the "duties of the defunct Cipher Bureau with those of the Cipher Compilation Service"; the forerunner of the Army Security Agency and of the National Security Agency.

It was autumn before details of the new organization were worked out and Friedman visited New York to supervise the packing and shipping to Washington of the Black Chamber's records.

Then he set about planning his new task. It was to have a lasting effect on him, as he was to admit years later. "You may be interested to know," he wrote to William Bundy, Henry Stimson's biographer, in discussing the work of the Black Chamber, "that my own feelings on the ethical point at issue are quite ambivalent — and have been for a long time. I have often wondered whether a good portion of my psychic difficulties over the years are not attributable, in part at least, to that ambivalence. Were it not for the fact that what I learned from my work in that segment of the whole field was applied very directly to improvements in our own systems, I am sure the psychic effect would have been much more serious."

Chapter Six

After the Black Chamber

THE SIGNAL INTELLIGENCE SERVICE set up under Friedman's control created the watershed of his career. Before, he had been the compiler of codes and ciphers for use in a war that seemed no more than a moderately remote possibility. He had followed the development of the cryptographer's art with all the enthusiasm of a devoted professional, exercising his brain on the problems that electromechanical ciphering machines offered, collecting historical examples from the cryptographic past, proud of his position in Washington as the man who knew more than anyone else about the subject. Yet a great deal of his work had only a minimal contact with the real problems of the world. Teapot Dome was one exception. There were others, many involving his wife who helped show the importance of code breaking and deciphering in crime preven-

Elizebeth Friedman's favorite photograph of her husband, at the time a major in the Army Signal Corps, 1934.

tion. Yet it was difficult to believe that the one-man department in the Munitions building was affecting the course of history or the fate of nations.

From 1930 onward the position began to change, and not only because Friedman was now responsible for operations of the covert kind previously carried out by Yardley's Black Chamber. The growth of radio communication, and with it the development of radio interception began to offer up a wealth of enciphered traffic whose collection was not dependent on cable tapping or similar questionable means. The "Mukden incident" of September, 1931, when the Japanese occupied the great Chinese city, and Japan's subsequent occupation of Manchuria, was soon providing operational messages between armies in the field and their headquarters which in content and in quantity were more useful than anything to which Friedman had devoted his powers in the 1920s. The Italians were preparing for their conquest of Abyssinia and their Washington embassy was soon reporting on reaction in the United States, a flurry of diplomatic messages whose number began to ease the problems of decipherment. Hitler's accession to power in 1933 and the subsequent German attempt to win influence in South America, an area of special concern to the United States, also provided numerous "dummy runs" for the wartime operations of the next decade. In addition, a new dimension was before long being given to the whole field of cryptography by the use of machinery, not to encipher messages as in the Enigma and its variations, but to solve them; in 1934 Friedman, who had already worked out methods of code compilation with the use of I.B.M. machines, managed to secure one for cryptanalytic work, a step into the future whose implications even he probably did not fully recognize. Thus throughout the 1930s the picture of a small dedicated band of specialists, working on the frontiers of knowledge, acquiring information which was vitally to affect the coming war, steadily comes into focus.

First, Friedman had to build up a staff. One difficulty has been underlined in an official account of the origins and development of his organization. "[These men]" it says, "were given to understand that the Signal Intelligence Service was seeking to establish a permanent corps of trained experts in cryptology and that no-one who was not disposed to make this his life work would be engaged. It was recognised that the specialised nature of the work and the fact that work of this kind does not have its counterpart in civilian affairs, would tend to make individual employees more and more dependent for a livelihood upon the continued security of tenure of his position in the War Department."

This meant that men who came into the S.I.S. were, for all practical purposes, mortgaging their future. They had, moreover, to be men so well qualified that they could pick and choose their jobs.

Friedman was exceptionally lucky, in April, 1930, not only in selecting his first three recruits but in inducing them to join him. They were Frank Rowlett, Abraham Sinkov and Solomon Kullback, three young math graduates who were offered the jobs after Friedman had personally inspected their records and decided they were the men for the task. His judgment was good. All three stayed with the S.I.S. and its successors for the rest of their professional lives. Soon after this recruitment, two more men were added, making a five-man team whose "peculiar talents for mathematics, oriental and classical languages, statistics, mechanics or philology," in the words of the official history, "laid the basis for the exact and arcane training they entered upon." In 1931 Lieutenant Mark Rhoades was assigned to Friedman for a year's training but at the end of it wrote a note to the chief signal officer saying that a year was not long enough in which to learn all there was to be learned about cryptography. He was kept in the S.I.S. for a further year, then became instructor for the next trainees. A Signal Intelligence School was set up and by the mid-1930s a small stream of army officers was being given a groundwork in scientific cryptanalysis.

The less dramatic work of the organization which Friedman was now building up still consisted of code compilation. This had been going on for years and his impact on it was merely to put it, earlier than might have otherwise been the case, on a proper scientific basis and to use for the work, the electric tabulating machines that by now were coming into more general use. In the early days, little was known about the best ways of employing the equipment, and there were comic moments. "At first," Solomon Kullback recalls, "when different methods of carding code-words were being experimented with, we would go into a closed room and throw 60,000 cards up in the air to get a random selection."

Eventually, tabulating machines began to show results and the official history of the section records that by the mid-1930s a code whose compilation had previously required the work of four operators for six weeks, could be compiled by one man in two days. The use of ancillary machine equipment also helped in actual production of the codes once they had been compiled, and in 1936 Friedman and his staff produced three editions of the field code for divisions, one military intelligence code and one staff code.

Running parallel with this routine work was the setting-up of the radio intercept stations that were to have such an impact on the war that lay only a few years ahead. In 1935, Lieutenant Rhoades led a radio detachment which set up a station in the Philippines. The following year Sinkov began to supervise the setting-up of a station at Quarry Heights in the Panama Canal Zone and Kullback did the same in Hawaii. Other stations were eventually started in San Francisco, Fort Sam Houston, Texas, and Fort McKinley in the Philippines. Intercepts also came from the First Radio Intelligence Company at Fort Monmouth, New Jersey. In addition there was an intercept station in Washington itself while some enciphered messages appear to have come from commercial channels.

Even by 1936 there were only about a dozen men working in the cryptographic service in Washington and Friedman at times was almost overwhelmed by the flood of messages which came in from both service and civilian sources. While America's potential allies were not entirely ignored, most of the effort was concentrated on attempts to decipher messages from Japan, Italy and Germany. Kullback dealt with German affairs, Sinkov with Italian while Friedman himself, assisted by Rowlett in the early days, turned to the Japanese.

Here the problems were complex. The language itself presented difficulties which did not exist with German, Italian, or, for that matter, with any other European language. They were compounded by the whole-hearted enthusiasm which the Japanese had lavished on their cryptographic effort, the number of codes rising to nearly a hundred by the 1940s. Thus there was *Shin,* a special logistics code; *Otsu,* a tactical code used for surface forces; *F* for air-to-ground communication; *J* for diplomats in Europe; *IC* for spies; *Hato* for use by the ministries of Foreign Affairs and of the army and navy; and *S* for merchant ships of more than a thousand tons. Most, moreover, were regularly kept up-to-date by changes.

In addition, Japanese ciphers were soon to suggest the influence of the German Enigma machine, a copy of which had been bought by the Japanese in 1934. Friedman knew as much as anybody outside Germany about what was possible with Enigma, and his papers in the Signal records contain page after page of his efforts to discover a method of deciphering Enigma messages. However, even the machine reported upon by the Dutch officer in 1926 appeared to produce virtually unbreakable messages, and that model was only the beginning. When Hitler came to power in 1933, sales of the Enigma machine were stopped and its further development taken over by the German Armed Forces. It thus became, well before the outbreak of the Second World War, the cryptographic backbone of the German war effort. The Japanese, moreover, had made their own improvements, transforming it into the most ingenious enciphering device in existence.

The Japanese problem would therefore have been difficult enough in any case. It was made more so by the fact that the Japanese, shortly before buying Enigma, had wiped the cryptographic slate clean, abandoning almost all their earlier codes and starting again from scratch. This alarming event, which took place just as Friedman's team was getting into its stride, was the direct result of a book by Herbert Yardley describing the work of the Black Chamber, which had been maneuvered into the Signal Intelligence Service in 1929. Yardley had in that year been given the chance of running the service but at a greatly reduced salary. He refused and for some while found it difficult to make ends meet. Then, in the spring of 1931, he wrote *The American Black Chamber,* and three expanded extracts from it which were published in the *Saturday Evening Post.* So great was the furor it created that two years later when it was learned he was to publish another book, *Secrets of Japanese Diplomacy,* an act was rushed through Congress which successfully prevented its publication.

On appearance of the *Post* articles Friedman immediately protested that one of the photographs accompanying them named the code used by the British Foreign Office and the British Ambassador in 1921. "It is obvious," he went on, "that not only does this photograph prove that the Military Intelligence Division was working upon British codes during peace time and had actually solved at least one, but also that the Division had access to the cables." It was not the only irritation for the man now running the Black Chamber's successor. "I was also especially irritated," he wrote to another officer, "by the references to the matter of breaking seals on diplomatic packages, because the less said about such things the better." It was all highly embarrassing.

Worst of all were revelations that the Americans had tapped and deciphered the vital Japanese messages between Tokyo and Washington instructing the Japanese delegates to the Washington conference on disarmament in 1921. The Americans had known from day to day, it was now revealed, which cards the Japanese were holding and which they had been told to play. As a direct result of Yardley's revelations the Japanese launched a major program in which its security methods and devices were changed. "Friedman," in the words of an official Signal Corps history, "found himself starting over again, with a task a hundred times more difficult."

His work in the aftermath of *The American Black Chamber* would have been more than enough to keep him and his colleagues busy even had they been allowed to concentrate on nothing else. However, that was far from being the case. There were leftovers from the First World War as when the authorities, pressing claims against Germany for the sabotage which had led to the huge Black Tom explosion in 1916, asked for the decipherment of certain messages. When an enciphered warning was found wrapped round a bomb which had failed to kill Senator Huey Long, the warning almost inevitably came to the Munitions Building for decipherment.

A regular stream of work also arrived on Friedman's desk from the law-enforcement agencies, the most dramatic example being a long message intercepted by the Ohio State Prison Service while being passed out by a prisoner. When decoded it was found to outline a mass-escape plot and to give details of how a hole was to be blasted in the prison walls and of how cars, guns and money were already being organized for the escapers. In September, 1935, the secretary of the Secret Service Detail in the White House sent for decoding a message found on a suspect and thought to refer to "Count" Victor Lustig, the head of a gang of counterfeiters who had just escaped from prison. Friedman decoded it, by return, and Lustig was rearrested two days later.

There were also the unexpected, offbeat, enquiries which took up time, as when the Smithsonian Institution asked for a list of the thousand commonest words in current English for burial in the Time Capsule at the New York World's Fair. There was the young army officer who insisted on seeing Friedman to describe an alleged cipher which he imagined he had uncovered in certain well-known literary works. After a good deal of thought Friedman felt obliged to write to the man's commanding officer: "After having a few minutes conversation I came to the quite definite conclusion," he wrote, "that he is suffering from a not uncommon form of mental aberration. I regard it therefore as my duty to bring this to your attention, so that a watch may be kept on his behaviour in order to avoid possible unpleasant results. [He] in other respects seems to be a most intelligent and well-educated gentleman, and it is therefore all the more distressing to note what appears to be an approaching break. I need hardly add that careful handling will perhaps be necessary."

Codes connected with buried treasure also cropped up regularly. Judging by Friedman's experience, few states seemed to be without it, and in most cases the gold, jewels or hard cash would be discovered only after solution of a series of encoded or enciphered messages. A variant was provided by the millionaire who died without making a normal will but left, instead, a series of code and cipher writings which his lawyers wanted turned into plaintext. Friedman did his best to oblige.

"My own career," his wife once said, "has been spotted with appeals and prayers for help in solving messages or maps of buried treasure, smuggled gold, or gems." Important among these was the Beale Treasure, 2 million dollars' worth of gold, silver and precious stones brought back from California, and alleged to have been hidden near Roanoke, Virginia, in 1821 by Thomas Jefferson Beale. Directions for its recovery were left in three coded letters and even before the end of the nineteenth century attempts had been made to decode the letters and discover the hiding place. Friedman was not surprised when approached by a visitor who wished to make a business contract with him. Friedman must of course guarantee not to reveal the solution of the messages to anyone else and would, as a reward, receive a percentage of whatever treasure was found. Six months later a second visitor approached with the same proposition and was much alarmed to learn that he had apparently been forestalled. Others were interested and thirty years later at least one man — a retired general — was still hoping to find the treasure.

Friedman worked on the messages, on and off, when he could find time, for a number of years. He had no success and friends who knew what he was doing often asked whether he thought any treasure really existed. "On Mondays, Wednesdays and Fridays, I think it is real," he replied. "On Tuesdays, Thursdays and Saturdays I think it is a hoax."

Not all of those who tried to invoke Friedman's help were successful, as a Washington paper discovered after its city editor pleaded for Friedman's assistance, and sent out a reporter with two coded messages which lacked both address and signature. "Great secrecy re origin and how obtained," Friedman noted. "I recognised messages as being a Department of Justice code and . . . saw that paper had 'stolen' messages in attempt to obtain a scoop." He made an excuse for not cooperating. Then he warned the Department of Justice that they had better change that particular code.

There were other occasions when diplomacy was needed. Thus in the spring of 1936 there arrived on his desk a letter to President Roosevelt written by Roosevelt's cousin, the Catholic clergyman William Hoffman. It had been passed by Roosevelt to his military aide, Colonel Watson, and then down through the Intelligence section to Friedman. "Would it be possible for you to send me an authorisation of the sort I have scribbled on the enclosed sheet, so that the next time I am in Washington I can really get on the inside of modern developments of cryptography in our army and navy?"

it asked. "Needless to say, you can count on my discretion and my honour."

The authorization asked for stated that Hoffman was a student of cryptography and went on to request that chief signal officers in the army and the navy would "talk with complete frankness and lack of reserve to him in regard to modern developments in this science [of cryptography], and to place at his disposal for study material generally considered 'confidential' or 'secret.' " By return, Friedman prepared a note for Colonel Watson "recommending that no such authority be granted and stating that Father Hoffman had already been given more than was usually given to a civilian and that information of this type is not given to commissioned officers unless their official duties require it."

Not content, Father Hoffman is reported to have made a second approach to Roosevelt, only to be met with Friedman's comment: "There are some things which I cannot divulge even to the President."

It was not only real codes and ciphers, practical or impractical, that intrigued him. Fictional cryptography as well as factual, was drawn into his net, and even science-fictional. Thus the review of a novel, *The Black Shadow,* was clipped and went into his files. The reason was the introduction into the story of "a certain minute organism, a sort of slug in appearance, which reproduces its species by the splitting into two of the parents, just as the amoeba does. You'll finally," continued the reviewer, "get an indefinite number of slugs all descended from the one parent and all — this is the important point — having a strong nervous sympathy with one another, so that each will conform to the movements of the others, no matter how widely they may be separated. Suppose one parent had a half dozen of these creatures, and someone else another half dozen. . . . The first six are arranged in a definite pattern: the others immediately conform. It is only necessary to have a pre-arranged code . . . and any message can be sent from any distance." It was,

Friedman commented on the clipping, the most bizarre of all the many cipher or code systems he had encountered in detective tales.

The man who had by this time become Washington's cryptographic "enquire within" contrasted strongly with the too-frequent image of the academic, or the scientist engaged in exotic work. The William Friedman who always appeared in the office punctually was very different from the shaggy, casual figure of popular legend. With two-tone shoes, trim suit and immaculate shirt and tie, he was a dapper figure whose smartness was increased by his neatly trimmed mustache.

His formality, perhaps more typical of Europe than of the United States, was carried through by the way in which he spoke and the manner in which he insisted on being addressed. Lambros Callimahos, who was later to work with him and who became in some ways his successor, has described how for some years after they met it remained "Captain Callimahos" and "Mr. Friedman." Eventually it became "Cal" and finally "Lambros" on one side; on the other it was still "Mr. Friedman." A very small number of his closest associates were allowed to call him "Bill." To the rest he was "Mr. Friedman" not only in his presence but when he was discussed. "I used to speak of him affectionately as 'Uncle Willie' — but certainly not in his earshot," Callimahos says. "The soubriquet caught on and became widespread and when he learned of it he was amused. But once, at a party, when the two of us were by ourselves and I called him 'Uncle Willie' I was immediately made aware of my impertinence. One did not take liberties with William F. Friedman."

There were many parties, often livened by cryptographic games. There was also a dinner at which the first course was concluded by presentation of a cryptogram which had to be solved before the address was revealed of the restaurant where the second course was to be eaten — and so on with the rest of the courses. This near-obsession with his craft — which led to cryptographic Christmas cards — was balanced by the utilitarian practice of home handy-work before it became fashionable. Friedman built with his own hands a swimming pool in his garden and converted an attic into a work-room for his son.

Outside the office, "shop" occupied virtually all his intellectual energy. Tennis kept him physically in trim, and on Sunday mornings he would often be seen playing on the White House court. A social round that he distinctly enjoyed warded off any tendency to become the recluse cryptographer and, during this period at least, kept him from thinking too deeply about whether the ends of his work justified the means. Yet his spare time was spent, almost exclusively, on research into cryptography's historical set pieces or on the cryptographic problems he was perpetually being asked to deal with privately.

Of these set pieces, the most intriguing concerned the Zimmermann telegram. Sent in code in January, 1917, by the German foreign secretary, Arthur Zimmermann, to the German minister in Mexico, the telegram urged a German-Mexican alliance that would come into operation if the Americans entered the war against Germany. The Mexicans, it was urged, should in those circumstances cross the American frontier, an act of aggression for which they would later be rewarded with parts of New Mexico, Texas and Arizona. To add insult to injury, one version of the telegram was sent by the Germans to their ambassador in Washington over the U.S. State Department's private wire, a facility which the Germans had been given to ease the presentation of any peace moves.

The Zimmermann telegram was intercepted and decoded by the British, then passed on to the Americans, and its publication, on March 1, did much to bring the United States into the war the following month. However, the full story of how the British obtained the plaintext of the message had never been told, and for one very good reason: that the British were intercepting and reading not only German but also American messages, a fact which played a significant part in the Zimmermann affair. Friedman had for long wanted to disentangle the complicated business. "I am back on the Zimmermann with a vengeance because it keeps me awake," he wrote in 1937 to Dr. Mendelsohn, Yardley's former colleague in the Black Chamber and by now at the City College of New York. "If I do a couple of hours on it in the evening I still keep thinking and the wheels go round. The draft which I will submit to you will be very much different from what you think and it will be much longer than your preliminary draft. I am wondering if this will not turn out to be love's labour lost because maybe the permission to publish will not be forthcoming."

His doubts were to be justified. A friend in the State Department, he wrote later to Mendelsohn, "says that in his opinion the State Department would not like to have this thing printed right now for reasons which are, I imagine, obvious to you. In a period when we have so few friends, it might be rather indelicate to put out something which might possibly be a bit of a strain on friendship. In the second place . . . my superiors have bluntly told me that my name must not appear in the public press, and the situation is, I am sorry to say, such that even if my name were merely sponsoring authorship of a song or article having to do not at all with cryptography, it would not make any difference. From this, you will gather that they are pretty jittery and want to keep quiet even the fact that there is such a thing as cryptography going on."

The jitteriness, the reluctance to admit that cryptography existed even while the radio-intercept network was growing, was no doubt due to the administration's bad conscience about the covert methods sometimes employed. Once let it be hinted at that gentlemen might once again be reading each other's mail and other questions might be asked, even questions about breaking seals on diplomatic packages, that subject on which, in Friedman's opinion, the less said the better. Another reason was that the S.I.S. was still the poor relation of the army. Despite the encouragement given following the official demise of the Black Chamber, the official record now makes clear what was suspected in the 1930s by only a select few and known to even fewer: that the U.S. cryptographic services were starved of men, money and materials by comparison with those in Europe. In such circumstances it was more comfortable to pretend that the need for them did not seriously exist.

Friedman felt this crippling hold on the money bags almost personally and did what he could to loosen it. One opportunity came when a New York lawyer wrote to the Office of the Chief Signal Officer. On behalf of a client he had, he said, bought for $100,000 the North American rights in a cipher machine invented some years earlier by Alexander von Kryha of Germany. In fact, when the machine had been put on the market in the 1920s Friedman had tried to buy one. The European agents had refused to consider selling less than a hundred and, commented Friedman: "Uncle Sam doesn't allow us to buy even one pig in one poke, let alone 100 pigs in 100 pokes all at one time." Nevertheless, he had eventually managed to secure a machine but soon realized that its operation was too slow for military purposes. In addition he was unimpressed by claims for the huge number of alphabets it could produce, knowing that this was only one factor in a cipher system's security and not, necessarily, the most important one.

The lawyer attempting to interest the army insisted that Kryha encipherments could not be broken. Friedman insisted, on the contrary, that the system was vulnerable. Eventually, on Friedman's prompting, the army agreed to accept a two-hundred-word statement enciphered on the machine and see what could be done with it.

One morning a letter enclosing a message of 1,135 letters therefore arrived in Friedman's office. Here it was date-stamped "Feb 24 AM 11:12." Beside the time, he wrote the words: "Commenced work, W.F.F." The message had been asked for in triplicate and

131

Friedman now handed a copy each to Rowlett, Kullback and Sinkov, together with instructions of what they were to do. He himself supervised their work until lunchtime when he went out for fifty minutes, a fact which he noted on the top copy of the message. Early that afternoon it was again put in the date-stamp and marked "Feb 24 PM 2:43." Beside the time, Friedman wrote: "Solved, W.F.F." He then dictated a letter, put in the post shortly afterwards together with the solved message, giving the cipher alphabets used and the initial position of the machine's toothed cipher wheel. The letter to the New York lawyer concluded with thanks for the opportunity he had afforded "for testing in a practical manner theoretical studies made some time ago."

Friedman's subsequent explanation of how the machine worked is an example of his skill in presenting a complicated process to the lay mind in understandable terms. "It is obvious," he began, "that this machine involved nothing more than the use of two basic or primary alphabets, the interaction of which can produce a maximum of 26 secondary, inter-related cipher alphabets. The cryptograms produced by the machine can be duplicated by the use of but two sliding strips of cross-section paper. The mechanisms of the machine, the clockwork, cipher-wheel, etc., merely govern the successive displacements or juxtapositions of the two primary alphabets, and the principal questions are these: (1) How irregular are the successive displacements; (2) Does the machine manifest periodicity, and if so: (3) How long is the period: (4) Are there such internal relations within the period to reduce a given cryptogram to monoalphabetic terms: (5) If the latter is true, what is the minimum length of cryptogram practically solvable?"

The simplicity of the explanation is typical of the man who once commented of a paper on "Isomorphism and Its Applications in Cryptanalysis," "the best thing that can be said about this is that it is a beautiful example of high-flown and florid language in the expression of very simple ideas."

Following the return of the Kryha messages to the highly disappointed lawyer, Friedman prepared a memorandum in which he noted that "the speed with which the solution was accomplished in this case shows what proper organisation, effective co-ordination and experienced direction of trained cryptanalysts can accomplish." It was a justified boast; and, as he had hoped, it eventually found its way to the desk of the deputy chief of staff, together with an accompanying note from the chief of military intelligence. This expressed the hope that it would be possible to meet the chief signal officer's requests "for development of his Signal Intelligence Section, personnel and funds for research and construction of the additional codes as per recent programs."

The era of the 1930s during which U.S. cryptographers were starved of funds was among the most inventively fertile of Friedman's life. It is unlikely that he had ever heard of Lord Rutherford's comment at the Cavendish Laboratory in Cambridge when ushering in the nuclear age: "We haven't much money so we must use our brains." Nevertheless, as the Signal Service was pleading for funds Friedman was busy patenting a family of his own devices eventually to be used in America's wartime crypto-systems.

In the 1920s, as a result of work on the A.T.&T. machine, he had filed his first three patents. One introduced a connection-changing switchboard in a teletype encipherment system for automatically enciphering and deciphering messages; a second replaced the multiplex principle with carrier frequencies, and a third replaced the short-stop principle with that of the modulated carrier. The following year he had devised, and patented, an alphabetical chart for composing two-letter differential code symbols for various purposes, and in 1932 he and a colleague had patented the mechanical basis for a cryptographic system using the Baudot encipherment principles, with a mechanism to be superimposed on the keyboard of a standard typewriter.

All of these were important. All were, to a lesser or greater extent, incorporated in cryptographic machines which the United States was to be making in large numbers in the early 1940s. Yet they were overshadowed by another clutch of inventions and devices which Friedman was to conceive during the later 1930s. Like the earlier inventions he had patented, they were not made as part of his official duties. Friedman the cryptologist enciphered or deciphered, made up army codes or suggested theoretical ways in which the codes of other countries might be read. Development was the task of the Signal Corps Laboratories at Fort Monmouth, New Jersey, and if others wished to take a hand with the work then that was their own private affair. Thus it was Friedman, not the army authorities, who formally applied for, and was granted, the patents. However, that was only one side of a curious coin; the other presented the fact that the patents, due to their nature, had to be secret. The devices that would have been worth thousands of dollars if exploited in the open market had to remain concealed, not for a year or so but, in practice, indefinitely.

This was particularly true of Friedman's work after 1932. In July, 1933, he filed a patent for what was called simply a cryptographic system. In fact it employed the basic invention of electric control of a set of cryptographic rotors in cascade — rotors connected in such a way, that is, that each one operated the next one in turn. It was followed in January, 1936, by a patent, the first of its kind, for electrically controlling the vibration of the rotors when they stopped. Then, a few months later, came the patent for a device in which the angular placement of a set of rotors in cascade was in turn controlled by another set of rotors, a device which was to be the heart of the Sigaba, one of America's most-used enciphering devices during the Second World War. The following year he produced something entirely different, a message-authenticating system which included a keyboard, a perforated card-control and an adding machine mechanism. It was important not only for itself but because it was the first example of an

I.B.M. card being used for cryptographic keying purposes.

These were only the more important of Friedman's patents. Others included two basic inventions in the cryptanalytic field — for deciphering rather than enciphering, that is — submitted to the Signal Corps Patent Board in April, 1937. So highly secret did the board consider them to be that it recommended that no patent applications should be filed at all. The board's recommendation was followed. But at least one of these two inventions was in use soon afterwards — and was still in use two decades later.

Many of Friedman's patents were to affect the development of large cryptographic equipment which if not limited entirely to headquarters could certainly not be used well forward in the field. The need for a small and reliable cipher machine for such purposes was increasingly apparent, and the chief signal officer was allocated $2,000 for its development. At the Signal Corps Laboratories, Fort Monmouth, the military director decided that technical guidance or help from the Signal Intelligence Service was unnecessary, and concentrated on the design of an all-mechanical machine that did not require electricity. When completed, it was passed to the S.I.S. for a test of its security, together with two short messages. These were handed over to Friedman with the machine, since it had to be assumed that on active service the machine might be captured. "One of the test messages was solved in about 20 minutes, the other took longer — 35 minutes," Friedman commented later. "This test brought an ignominious end to the S.C.L. development, brought about by the failure on the part of the military director to recognise that cryptographic invention must be guided by technically qualified cryptanalytic personnel. Unfortunately, all the available funds had been expended on this unsuccessful attempt; none was left for a fresh start on a development with technical guidance from the S.I.S."

Eventually, the situation was restored by Boris Hagelin, but only after the European war had started, an event for which Friedman had been preparing himself since the time of Munich, when he seems to have had more forethought than his superiors. At the height of the crisis, he wrote to his friend Dr. Mendelsohn, asking if he could obtain leave of absence for six months if called upon to help the army in an emergency. "I don't want you to think that this question is now being asked you indirectly by my own superiors," Friedman had added. "I am anticipating that they may ask me such a question, and I would like to have some idea of your probable reply."

Even before Munich the army's clampdown on any mention of cryptography had been increased. The results were sometimes ludicrous, as when Friedman was smartly called over the coals for speaking to a small specialist audience about the decipherment of Egyptian hieroglyphics. There was also the case of his article in the *Signal Corps Bulletin* on "Jules Verne as Cryptographer." The Jules Verne Society obtained a copy of the *Bulletin* and wished to review the article in their journal. But this was not possible. "It may seem rather stretching things a bit," the author told the editor of the *Journal,* "but in view of the fact that the article appears in a War Department publication of the 'Restricted' category, material contained therein is not available to the public, and, therefore a review of my article in a public journal would be out of order."

Three months after Munich Friedman returned from an inspection trip to Panama and Honolulu. As far as friends and acquaintances were concerned, it was merely a "jaunt," undertaken as much for health reasons as for anything else, and he came back, as his wife wrote to friends, "having gained some weight and very brown." He had, in fact, been helping to tie in the details of an important reorganization initiated by General Mauborgne. Until now the detachments in the Canal Zone, Texas, San Francisco, Hawaii and the Philippines had functioned under the signal officers of their various corps areas or departments. Now they were brought under the wing of a single unit, the Second Signal Service

Company at Fort Monmouth, which before the year was out was operating an additional intercept station in Virginia. The company headquarters was moved to Washington and given quarters next to Friedman's S.I.S.

With the setting-up of the new group, a response to the looming threat of a European war, there came a further tightening-up of cryptographic security. As a start, the authorities in Washington bought from the Riverbank Laboratories all remaining copies of Friedman's papers which had been published there. Even at this late date, so little information on the subject was available in the United States that the papers of twenty years earlier fell into the category "of use to an enemy." Surprisingly, even when the Bell Telephone Laboratories reasonably enough asked the War Department for copies, they received only a dusty answer. "I don't see any need for them in telegraph work," Friedman replied personally, "and suspect that the librarian has been asked by somebody to get these publications for personal study."

Chapter Seven

Challenge

The Breaking of Purple

DECIDING WHO SHOULD have copies of such papers as "The Index of Coincidence" was a rather minor worry in the spring of 1939. Friedman's teams had achieved partial success with the Italian and German code-systems and some also with the Japanese Army systems, while their naval counterparts were already managing to read a number of the Japanese naval codes. But there was also "Purple," the Japanese diplomatic cipher-system used by the Foreign Office in Tokyo for the most secret communications with its ambassadors abroad.

Purple — usually known as the Purple Code even though it was a cipher — has become the most famous encipherment system not only in the history of cryptography but also in its mythology and folklore. There are many interlocking reasons for this. The most obvious is that it was probably more complex than any system

138

devised before the days of electronic computers and that its solution involved a unique intellectual effort of heroic proportions. Another reason for its fame is the spectacular way in which the news of its existence was given in the U.S. congressional hearing into the Pearl Harbor disaster. During the following years its fame was compounded as first one and then another example came to light showing how the breaking of Purple had influenced the war in the Pacific. If this was not enough to give Purple a unique place in the annals of cryptography there was a later revelation; that as a direct result of the breaking of Purple the Americans knew, before the dropping of the atomic bombs on Hiroshima and Nagasaki that the Japanese were putting out peace feelers. To all this there was added the curious reluctance of either Americans or British to discuss the effect of Purple on the war in Europe — far greater than has ever been publicly revealed — or the way in which Anglo-U.S. cryptographic cooperation enabled which ally to use what intercepts for specific purposes.

Friedman and his team in the Munitions Building began receiving intercepts in Purple soon after it came into use in 1937. In one way they were lucky. When Herbert Yardley's book on the Black Chamber had been published six years earlier and the Japanese had immediately scrapped their existing codes and hurriedly sought for something more secure, the change was considered an unqualified disaster. However, it was later realized that there might be another way of looking at the situation. The Japanese might well have waited until the edge of war in 1941 before they changed their more important codes. "In that case," wrote one of Friedman's colleagues years later, "I'm afraid that the end results might well have been different although Uncle Willie possibly has a different view." In other words, the Americans could have spent the first year or two of war struggling to break open the Japanese system — all the while ignorant of their enemy's plans. As it was, the position was startlingly different.

The messages that Friedman began to receive in Purple in 1937 were less numerous than those in most of the other Japanese ciphers and it was some while before they began to comprise enough material for any attempted decipherment. When they did so the S.I.S. was unpleasantly surprised. It had been taken for granted that Purple was a machine encipherment; in the nature of things it was likely the German Enigma machine would be involved. What the Americans were hardly prepared for was the wealth of ingenious development work that had multiplied the difficulties of deciphering any Enigma system.

The Japanese had started with the machine bought for the Imperial Navy. But before putting it into use a number of ingenious improvements and adaptations had been incorporated. So successful were they that it was some while before the U.S. naval cryptographers had begun to work their way into the Japanese naval code known as the Red system. Then, shortly after they had begun to unravel the complexities of Red, which was also used for many diplomatic messages, a new system, exclusively diplomatic and therefore an army responsibility, began to take over.

What had happened was that the Imperial Navy had turned over their adapted Enigma system to the Foreign Office and the Foreign Office cryptographers had added their own clever modifications to it. The result was 97-shiki-O-bun In-ji-ki or Alphabetical Typewriter 97, the last two figures signifying year 2597 of the Japanese calendar. This end product was radically different not only from the Enigma machine which had given it birth but also from Hagelin's Swedish machines, from the American Sigaba which Friedman was to help produce, and from the eventual British counterpart.

The physical basis of the Purple machine was a battery of standard six-level, twenty-five-point "off-the-shelf" stepping switches plus a standard commercial plugboard and an intricate system of wiring. The Japanese operator sat down before the first of two typewriters representing the input and output equipment. He then had to consult a book which told him the particular key or keys to be used on that day, and plug up the plugboard accordingly. Next he had to turn the rotors until each stood in the position indicated for the code of the day. In a later improvement of the machine, he had the choice of two codes for each day, one for normal use and one for a further super-encipherment used only for messages of extraordinary secrecy and importance.

That all done, he tapped out the message on the typewriter, using for any numerals, which were not handled by the machine, a three-letter code-word which was enciphered in the same way as the rest of the message. Simultaneously, the enciphered message appeared on the second typewriter.

The first step in what seemed to be the impossible task of decipherment lay in collecting a certain minimum of traffic sent on one day — or, at least, sent with the same keys in operation, which was initially the same thing. The next step was to decide which permutation and combination of wiring could have been used to produce such a set of enciphered messages. If the decision was correct all messages sent on that particular day could be deciphered to produce intelligible plaintext. If not, not; and for month after month it was always not.

Gradually, however, fragmentary parts of a possible solution began to be built up. From the start of 1939 the navy cryptologists began to help. For one thing they took over the work on all Japanese diplomatic systems other than Purple, thus allowing Friedman and his staff to concentrate on what was by now being appreciated as the most important of all contemporary cryptographic riddles. They passed on all their own Purple intercepts. More important, they handed over to the army all the technical information on the standard solution of the Red system and on the techniques which had been used for finding it. There were enough similarities between the two systems for this to be useful —

but still enough differences for the unraveling of Purple to remain a unique challenge.

Early in 1939 there came a radical change in the tempo of attack. Credit for it must go to General Mauborgne, who realized that progress on Purple was so slow as to offer little prospect of eventual success unless something drastic was done. One reason for this, he correctly believed, was that Friedman himself had throughout the previous eighteen months been largely occupied with administrative duties. He had suggested lines of attack, studied results, made recommendations; but the bulk of his time and his thought had been devoted to the multiplicity of day-to-day problems that had to be solved if Sigaba was to be brought into effective operation, if the American forces were to have efficient encipherment systems for use in the field should war come. Like a leading research scientist who is slowly pushed up the ladder of success until, as director of a national institution, he begins to lose touch with research, Friedman had been sidetracked from the work of which he was master. In February, 1939, General Mauborgne therefore ordered him to drop all other activities. The solution of Purple must come first.

Friedman now began the most acute eighteen months of intellectual effort he was ever to undertake. His problem was to discern, in the jumble of enciphered letters, some regularities that would lead him on to discover the laws under which these regularities had been brought into existence. The task was not unlike that which Einstein faced in trying to find the regularities which revealed the natural laws of the universe, or which Crick and Watson tackled in unraveling the secrets of the genetic code embodied in DNA. There was, however, one great difference. As Einstein said in describing his efforts to discover God's laws, "God is subtle but he is not malicious." He may make it difficult for man to fathom the laws of the universe but will not be perverse in His manner of concealment. With cryptographers, the case is different. Every trick of the trade will be used to prevent the outsider from looking in.

Apart from the Red solutions, a few things helped the men in the Munitions Building. There were certain forms of address to be expected at the head of messages to certain destinations. At times, certain subjects seemed likely to occur in diplomatic messages and the possibility of certain enciphered words representing specific plaintext words could be tested. Very occasionally the State Department might have the plaintext of a message which had been intercepted, partly or completely, in cipher, thus providing further clues to that particular day's keys. Less frequently, a Japanese operator might repeat the mistake of the German operator on the day that the ADFGVX cipher had been introduced in 1918, and duplicate a Purple message in an outdated code which the Americans had already broken.

All such items enabled fresh theories to be tested and even though they were found wanting, the work was not useless. As Einstein himself had said after working for years on a unified field theory that came to nothing: "This means that no-one need now waste his time on this theory."

Throughout this period, Friedman worked under a veil of secrecy that prevented him from mentioning the subject even to his wife, helpful though her ideas might well have been. He departed regularly for the Munitions Building each morning and returned regularly each evening. There was only one change in his habits. Now, in the early hours of the morning, he would often get up, go down to the kitchen, make himself coffee and sandwiches, and then be heard pacing back and forth for hour after hour.

This went on throughout the long hot summer of 1939, and throughout the autumn as the German tanks rolled across the Polish plains and Poland itself was sliced up between Hitler's Germany and Stalin's Soviet Union. Success began to come slowly the following spring and summer as first Norway then France and the Netherlands fell to the Wehrmacht, and from Cap Gris Nez Goering gazed across a mere twenty-two miles of water to the white cliffs of Dover.

Then, as the Luftwaffe began its assault on the airfields of southern England, in August, 1940, Friedman and his team achieved the first vital breakthrough. A suggestion came from Larry Clark, a young civilian cryptanalyst who had been recruited by Friedman in the early 1930s. Why, he asked himself, should the Japanese not have used something different from the discs that had been the rotors in the earlier machines? Whether, as reported, he had said: "I wonder if the monkeys did it that way," is a moot point. What is certain is that Friedman quickly exploited the idea. Within a few days a number of partial solutions had been found. Now, moreover, they could set about building a mock-up of the Japanese machine.

Ironically, the first major ungarbled solution of a Purple message came on September 25, 1940, just two days before Germany, Italy and Japan signed in Berlin the Tripartite Pact pledging all three of them to mutual support, an event which led to an unexpected, but useful, cascade of Purple messages.

That night, remembers Elizebeth, her husband returned home as usual, without any sign that the great job had been done.

A good many legends have grown around the building by Friedman and his colleagues of the machine which imitated the Japanese Purple device. It was, in fact, made from electrical equipment in short supply. It was not elegant, and from all accounts it appears to have replicated the Japanese machine not only in its ability to encipher and decipher, but in the showers of sparks which it sometimes gave off when operated. Strangely enough, the Americans who so brilliantly constructed this hardware from their theoretical conclusions, were never to see how like or unlike the original their duplicate really was. As war broke out between Japan and the United States, the Japanese in the Washington embassy hammered their Purple machine to pieces. When a British regiment took over

Japan's Berlin embassy in May, 1945, the Japanese, or the Russians, had already removed all cryptographic equipment. The same was true throughout the Far East, including Tokyo itself, as the Americans began their occupation in the summer of 1945. A few broken metal parts were all that Friedman or his colleagues ever saw of Japan's Purple machine.

The solution of the enciphering processes and the reconstruction of the Japanese machine were superb achievements. However, cryptography being what it is, this did not automatically lead to the easy reading of all diplomatic messages. It was still necessary to collect sufficient messages in one key before that key could be found and then used for decipherment. Nevertheless, the teams working on Purple were eventually able to predict about 90 percent of the Purple keys before they were used, the result of a major breakthrough by a young naval officer, Lieutenant Francis A. Raven. He had come into the picture after it had been decided that, to ease the work load, naval cryptanalysts would handle Purple messages on odd days of the month and the army should do the same on even days. Raven's discovery was that the Japanese had divided the month into thirds, and that the keys used in each ten-day third were usually jugglings of the keys used on the first day of each section. The solutions for the first, eleventh, and twenty-first of the month still had to be found but the keys for the succeeding nine days could in most cases then be revealed with much less trouble.

There were other bottlenecks which qualified the use which could be made of the breaking of Purple. One was caused by the purely physical delay in passing on intercepts to the cryptographers. Hawaii, for instance, sent an accumulated packet of intercepts to Washington once a week by commercial air clipper, or by ship if the clipper was delayed by bad weather. Only those messages which fell into special categories laid down by the chief signal officer were radioed to Washington. To such delays were added those caused by the fact that a small number of men had to handle a huge volume of traffic which was received in a large number of systems. These were first sorted into priority groups, with Purple at the top. Then the cryptanalysts had to obtain the key. While this would sometimes take only fifteen minutes or so, it might occasionally take a week or a month, while some keys were never recovered at all. Cryptanalysts did not grow on trees and in spite of the expansion of both Friedman's department and its navy equivalent, it is true that throughout the entire war far too many messages were finding their way on to the desks of far too few cryptanalysts.

There was also the further delay provided by translation. Few Japanese-speaking Americans were available and fewer still fulfilled the super-stringent security qualifications demanded. Yet even when the cryptanalysts had deciphered an individual message there was no method of knowing its importance, or even what it was about, until it had been at least quickly scanned by a translator. Only then was it possible to arrange the Purple messages in their own order of priority.

In spite of these facts, which limited the full exploitation of the U.S. Army's unique cryptanalytic success, Friedman had with his colleagues now forged for the government an invaluable tool which was to change the course of history. By the autumn of 1940 there was available for the State Department, and for the Chiefs of Staff, a continuing flow of top secret information from Tokyo in which the Japanese leaders outlined their plans for the future and the strategy and tactics with which they were to be carried out.

Friedman himself was to have no control over the way in which this tool was used. He was a loyal man and, publicly at least, he did not complain. Yet there is ample evidence in his papers that during the next few years he was bitterly distressed at the apparent inability of many politicians and some servicemen to use the new tool effectively.

The successful breaking of Purple in the late summer of 1940 came some four months after the German occupation of western

Europe, a steamroller success which had brought Boris Hagelin to the United States. The event was to have a dramatic impact on the development of American cryptography.

Hagelin's B-21 machine, and its more sophisticated sister, the motor-driven B-211, had eventually been sold to a number of countries. But in the early 1930s a demand for a "pocket" version arose, and in 1934 Hagelin had invented one, completely mechanical in function, which was destined to become the most widely sold ciphering machine. Friedman and Hagelin kept in close contact regarding its development, but it was only in 1937 that Hagelin visited Friedman in Washington and demonstrated it to him and his colleagues. The discussions were mostly exploratory, but the meeting was the start of a friendship between Friedman and Hagelin which lasted until Friedman's death.

In the summer of 1939 Hagelin visited Washington again, bringing with him a crude prototype similar to the pocket machine but electrically operated. But everyone by now seemed more concerned with the crisis in Europe, Hagelin returned to Sweden when Germany invaded Poland and the Second World War began, and nothing appeared to have come of the visit.

Seven months later, when the Germans invaded Denmark and Norway, Hagelin decided to go to the United States with his pocket machine — which had by this time been provided with a base plate and a protective cover which made it easily portable. However, there were difficulties. The first arose when he arrived in Stockholm from a visit to his country home in the north and found it impossible to obtain a normal visa. The problem was overcome by persuading the Swedish foreign office to send him to the United States as a diplomatic courier and thus enable him to obtain a diplomatic passport. Some weeks passed before these formalities were completed, and Hagelin and his wife were ready to leave only on that day in May when the Germans began to invade France and the Low Countries. All sailings for the United

States, they found, had temporarily been canceled.

Hagelin now made an audacious decision. With him he had not only two ciphering machines of the B-21 type but also a set of manufacturing blueprints. He was determined that these should be delivered to America and he decided that the only remaining chance of getting them there was to sail from Italy. However, this meant traveling across the length of Germany, with the machines and the blueprints, covered by nothing more than the slender security of a diplomatic courier's bag.

He took the chance. He and his wife traveled by way of Berlin and Vienna and arrived in Genoa three days later. By this time, Italy's entrance into the war was imminent and the Hagelins finally reached New York on the *Conte di Savoia,* the last ship from Genoa.

In Washington he conferred with Friedman. It was decided that fifty more enciphering machines were needed for testing and these were successfully smuggled out of Sweden and arrived in Washington in September.

Friedman, as technical director of the Signal Intelligence Service, was asked to report. "I turned in an unfavourable report on the machine for the reason that although its crypto-security was theoretically quite good, it had a low degree of security if improperly used," he said later, "and practical experience had taught me that improper use could be expected to occur with sufficient frequency to jeopardise the security of all messages enciphered by the same setting of the machine, whether correctly enciphered or not. This was because the Hagelin machine operates on what is termed the key-generator principle, so that when two or more messages are enciphered by the same key stream, or portions thereof, solution of those messages is a relatively simple matter. Such solution permits recovery of the settings of the keying elements so that the whole stream can be produced and used to solve messages which have been correctly enciphered by the same key settings, thus making a whole day's traffic readable by the enemy." Although Friedman tried to assure his superiors that he was not moved by the "NIH" — "not invented here" — factor, he was overruled. "Quite properly," he says, "because neither the Signal Intelligence Service nor the Signal Corps Laboratories at Fort Monmouth had developed anything that was better than the Hagelin machine or even as good." However, he did recommend certain further im- improvements. These were made and by 1942 the Smith-Corona Typewriter Company of Groton, New York, was turning out hundreds of the machines. By the end of the war some 140,000 had been made.

How Purple Came to Britain

The Friedman team's success with Purple in August and September, 1940, had come at an interesting moment in military cryptography quite apart from the arrival in Washington of Hagelin and his equipment.

In Britain, which had been at war with Germany since the previous September, and with Italy since May, some formidable feats of cryptanalysis had already been accomplished. Between the two world wars the government's Code and Cipher School — or the Golf Club and Chess Society as it was flippantly called — set up in Broadway, Westminster, in 1923 under Commander Denniston and combining the functions of Yardley's Black Chamber, Friedman's Signal Intelligence Service, and the U.S. naval counterpart, had achieved a mixed record of failure and success. In 1927, when the government's inept move against the Russian trading organization had revealed that at least some Russian codes had been broken, these were scrapped by the Russians and replaced by use of the one-time pad, a system which although it had operational disadvantages was virtually unbreakable. Eight years later the Abyssinian War gave Denniston the opportunity for which he had been waiting, and a number of Italian codes were broken following efficient interception of Italian naval traffic off East Africa. But there was a price to be paid: the Germans, radio-watching British naval vessels in the Red Sea just as the British were watching the Italians, accumulated enough intercepts to break some of the Admiralty's codes. The Germans exploited their success and by the outbreak of the Second World War their Beobachtungdienst B-Dienst in Berlin had fifty cryptanalysts reading British naval codes alone, an operation that continued successfully until 1942–1943.

Two years after Abyssinia, the Spanish Civil War, in which the Italians used their own adaptation of Enigma to service their interventionist forces, gave the British a chance to study their machine encipherments. This time Denniston's team had little success. However, by August, 1939, when they had been evacuated to Bletchley, a small town some forty miles north of London, the British had obtained at least one, and possibly two, replicas of the German Enigma machine, altered and improved for use by the German services.

It is typical of the contradictions surrounding the cryptographic establishment that there are two different versions of how it, or they, were secured. According to General Bertrand of the French cryptographic services — who has described the events in his book *Enigma* — the French were in the 1930s able to supply their Polish allies with certain Enigma material bought from a civilian cipher clerk in the German Army. The Poles, who had already made some progress in breaking the Enigma systems, were then able to complete their work, and to reconstruct the new Enigma mechanism — a feat somewhat comparable to that of Friedman's team on Purple but one of course made infinitely easier by use of the German Army material. On January 9, 1939, French, Polish and British cryptologists met in Paris and discussed the problems that still remained, since having a replica of the machine was only a part of the solution. The Poles now took over the theoretical side of the remaining work while the British concentrated on the practical problem: that of discovering how best to find out which particular setting of the machine had been used to encipher any specific intercept. They all met again in July, this time near Warsaw, and according to Bertrand, the Poles then handed over their copy of the up-to-date Enigma. Shortly afterwards the French and the British each had two models.

According to *The Ultra Secret,* Group-Captain Winterbotham's account of the vital part that the Enigma decipherments played in winning the war in Europe, a Polish mechanic working on Enigma for the Germans was persuaded by the French to build a replica of the machine in Paris. All that this did, however, was to convince the British that an actual machine must somehow be secured. The feat was achieved by the Poles, to whom the operation was, as it were, contracted out, and in the summer of 1939 Denniston triumphantly returned from Poland to Britain with one of the latest, electrically operated Enigmas. Whatever the details — which may well include actions by the anti-Nazi "resistance" in Germany which it is not yet expedient to reveal — it is certain that by September, 1939, the British had a working machine. Before them there still lay the task of determining which of the countless variations of permutation and combination the enemy was using in any one set of intercepted messages. By early April, 1940, much of the job had been done, largely through the work of "Dilly" Knox, brother of the Catholic polemicist and amateur cryptographer Ronald Knox, and Alan Turing, a young mathematical genius. Turing had built what with only slight inaccuracy can be called the world's first electronic computer, "the Bronze Goddess" with whose use the complexities of the German crypto-systems based on Enigma could be unraveled at speed. The result was that throughout the crisis summer of 1940 the British were reading many of the most secret operational messages of the Wehrmacht and the Luftwaffe.

The work in Britain paralleled Friedman's in more than one way. It was not only an intellectual achievement of high order; it was also an operation carried out at such a level of secrecy that its details, in fact its very existence, was kept from all except those Allied commanders directly affected, as well as from well-wishers in Roosevelt's United States. If the cryptologists of the Signal Intelligence Service had throughout 1939 acted as though their massive interception and deciphering effort did not exist — in contrast to the flood of reports and scientific papers on nuclear weapons then being published in the United States — the British had kept their own secrets even more closely to themselves. Yet cryptology, almost more than any other subject, was one which demanded not only the intuitive genius of a Friedman or an Alan Turing but the plodding accumulation of data from as many sources as possible. The whole was invariably greater than the sum of its individual parts, and if any field of military endeavor called for cooperation between allies or potential allies it was the business of reading the enemy's messages.

Yet only in the summer of 1940, as Friedman struggled to the point of intellectual collapse with the recalcitrant Purple, were the first tentative steps taken towards cryptologic cooperation, measures later to be the object of virulent political attack, and a significant feature of the debate which followed the Pearl Harbor disaster.

Earlier in the summer, as the German armies overran western Europe and Britain faced the prospect of invasion, Roosevelt and Churchill had signed the famous destroyers-for-bases deal. Under this agreement, Britain granted the United States ninety-nine-year leases on ground in Bermuda to be used for naval and air bases, while the United States supplied in return destroyers, which were soon being used to reinforce protection of the vulnerable British convoys crossing the Atlantic.

Early in July Lord Lothian, the British ambassador in Washington, met Roosevelt to propose still further, and even more important, cooperation. Britain had by this time not only developed radar but had, even before the start of the war, set up an early warning system that was now, in the summer of 1940, helping the Royal Air Force in its defense of the skies above southern England. The Germans had quite independently developed their own radar system but had failed to integrate it with Luftwaffe operations, thus wasting the greater part of its potential value. They had, moreover, failed to solve the technical problems of shortwave radar, a development essential to the airborne radar devices soon to play such a vital role in the Allied bombing offensives. As far as America was concerned the development of radar, whose principles had been known since Marconi used a primitive radar device in the 1920s to avoid collisions at sea, was in its early stage. A number of academics, notably Alfred Loomis, chairman of the National Defense Research Committee on Microwaves, was by the late summer of 1940 experimenting with some fairly primitive devices. But nowhere in the United States had any steps been taken towards a warning system. Indeed, with the Atlantic and the Pacific separating them from potential enemies, there was little reason why they should have been. Nevertheless, those who viewed the world scene impartially saw America's interests as increasingly threatened by the Berlin-Rome Axis — and by the policies of Tokyo — and knowledge of Britain's technological achievement became increasingly desirable.

At this point Lothian saw Roosevelt, and on Churchill's instructions proposed that the British should reveal to the Americans details of their latest technological secrets, primarily those of radar but also others covering proximity fuses, submarine detection and radio interception. "Should you approve the exchange of information," Lothian wrote to the President on July 8, "it has been suggested by my Government that, in order to avoid any risk of the information reaching our enemy, a small secret British mission consisting of two or three Service officers and civilian scientists should be despatched immediately to this country to enter into discussions with Army and Navy experts."

At this stage the British offer was unqualified. Nothing was asked for in return although looking back across a third of a century it is quite clear that the offer was a well-dangled sprat designed to catch a very big mackerel. "His Majesty's Government," said Lothian's Aide-Memoire on the subject, "would greatly appreciate it if the United States Government, having been given the full details of any British equipment or devices — would reciprocate by discussing certain secret information of a technical nature, which our technical experts are anxious to have, urgently."

Thus was the stage set for the Tizard Mission, which after preliminary talks with the Canadians arrived in Washington in August. It was led by Sir Henry Tizard, the man most responsible for pushing Britain's radar defenses through the barriers of bureaucratic noninterest which had persisted almost to the outbreak of war. Unofficial adviser to the air ministry, Sir Henry, who came with a mixed service-civilian party as Lothian had suggested, probably knew more about scientific-military developments than any other man alive. The equipment which he brought to the United States certainly justified his reputation, including as it did the world's first cavity magnetron, the small piece of equipment that was the key to shortwave radar.

Tizard's brief did not include items of cryptographic importance, and it is likely that he knew no more than the barest details of what had been achieved at Bletchley, so tight was the security covering its activities. But on August 27, Tizard had a meeting with General Mauborgne. "We were to have only a few minutes talk," he wrote in his diary, "but he got interested and went on until lunch time."

It seems likely that Tizard and Mauborgne talked mainly, if not exclusively, about radar and no direct link has been traced between the meeting and the events in the cryptographic field which followed in the autumn. Yet it is difficult to believe that the germ of cryptographic cooperation was not in some way the result of the morning's talk. Certainly the climate that was to make such cooperation possible was a direct result of Tizard's talks with American diplomatic and service leaders.

Sir Henry returned to Britain with his colleagues early in October. Soon afterwards, agreement for further scientific cooperation was signed as formally as was possible between a Britain fighting for her life and a neutral United States. Thus far, there was no direct proposal for the interchange of cryptographic secrets. Indeed, neither side would have seen much point in such an exchange. The Americans, confident that they had the Japanese cryptographic problem well in hand, did not know that the British had won the Battle of Britain not only with the help of radar but with the help of Enigma decipherments. The British, equally confident that they had mastered many of the German codes — but not the German submarine codes which were solved only at the last minute of the last hour as the Battle of the Atlantic was reaching its climax — had for their part no knowledge of the American success with Purple.

The break that was to lead to cooperation came in October, 1940, and both Americans and British are distinctly shy of admitting details; the Americans because of the political repercussions, the British because of their congenital reserve. However, it is virtually certain that the British learned of the American Purple breakthrough in October, 1940. Major General G. V. Strong of the Army War Plans Division, who paid a brief visit to England in September, 1940, and who returned to London the following month on permanent duty, has been named as the man responsible and Americans tend to regard the incident as, according to their politi-

cal view of the Roosevelt administration, wise if belated cooperation or a disaster.

Strong was in London as the army representative of the Joint
(Army-Navy) Board, and his title of Special Observer put him on
higher ground than the regular military attachés. Just what happened is not known. But to Strong, as to other informed observers,
it was obvious by October, if not before, that the Germans could
no longer win command of the air over southern England. Without
that, invasion by the Germans would almost certainly be a military
disaster for them. And if there were to be no successful German
invasion, the German victory could only come, if it came at all, by
the long slow strangulation of British supplies from the United
States. The war, it now seemed certain, would be going on for a
long while yet, and the chances that America herself would eventually be drawn in were substantially increased.

In these circumstances, with so much now hanging on the con-
tinuation of American supplies from across the Atlantic, it would
be natural for the British to divulge to the nearest American with
the greatest potential military influence, one more important secret: the fact that victory of "the Few" in the Battle of Britain had
been won with the help not only of radar but of the plaintext
messages of German operational orders, deciphered with the help
of Enigma. General Strong, also looking to the future, would have
found it natural to reveal, in return, that the Americans had done
with Purple what the British had done with Enigma. The details
of any such disclosures are still unrevealed; and whether the British
would have again been dangling a sprat to catch a mackerel is a
moot point. What seems to be evident is that by mid-October the
British knew that the Americans had broken the most important
of the Japanese cipher-systems; and it is certain that before the end
of the next month an agreement had been signed by Britain and the
United States involving a full exchange of cryptographic systems.
The Americans were to get the keys needed for the decoding and

deciphering of the latest German systems, and the machinery for using such keys; the British were to get one of the Purple machines by this time being built in Washington.

Friedman had no part in the negotiations that led to this exchange. Neither did he put his views on record, either at the time or later. But from November onwards he became directly involved in preparations for the mission it was planned he would lead to England, a sort of cryptographic Tizard mission in reverse, "for the purpose of establishing technical co-operation with the British cryptanalytic service."

He was to be accompanied to Bletchley by two army officers and two navy officers and he was to take a mixed bag of cryptographic material whose details have never been officially disclosed. The secrecy is not only due to American reluctance to spell out the extent of the neutral United States aid to wartime Britain; there is also the extreme secrecy covering the aftermath of Friedman's successful operation on Purple and the problems involved in building replicas of the Japanese machine.

The first replica was kept for use by the U.S. Army while others were being built. Just how many others has never been stated, but it seems that by the end of 1941 eight in all were available. Number One was retained in Washington and Numbers Two and Three were assigned to the mission to England, one going to Bletchley and the other to the Admiralty. The fourth was retained in Washington by the navy, and the fifth was sent to the Philippines, at first to Cavite and finally to the famous communications tunnel on Corregidor. The sixth and seventh models were kept in Washington for use as spares while the eighth was sent to London in the early autumn of 1941. None, it was later pointed out, went to Pearl Harbor, the American naval base in Hawaii, and one of the most important American targets in the world; a lack of clear thinking at the top, rivalry between the army and the navy, and a dangerous assumption that no one would really attack the United States, stand out as the main reasons for what, at least with hindsight, appears to have been a staggering omission. Conspiracy, the stand-by argument of the revisionists who claim that Roosevelt egged on the Japanese to attack, comes far down the list of possibilities.

Late in October, 1940, Friedman was promoted to full colonel in preparation for the all-important visit to England; but his papers had not come through when, on December 23, after a fresh medical examination, he was put on active duty. Less than a fortnight later he collapsed. The strain of the previous 18 months had at last exacted its penalty and on January 4, 1941, he was taken to the neuro-psychiatric ward of the army's Walter Reed General Hospital.

He was, most strangely in view of the reason for his breakdown, put in a ward with between sixteen and twenty other patients. "There was," says Elizebeth Friedman, who was allowed to spend the major part of each day with him, "only one psychiatrist for them all, so that discussions etc. were not individual. In other words, the patient was isolated except for his fellow-patients, who could discuss and consult with each other if they felt inclined to do so." Eventually, it was diagnosed that he was suffering from extreme nervous fatigue "due to prolonged overwork on a top secret project."

In mid-January a team of two army officers and two navy officers with two Purple machines, and a variety of other cryptographic equipment, crossed the Atlantic. This was only the first installment. By the end of 1941 London had received two Red machines, copies of those used by Japanese naval attachés, and two J–19s, one of each later being forwarded by the British to Singapore. In due course — although only after a delay which was politically ascribed to treachery but was largely the result of misunderstanding — Washington received the results of the vital British work on Enigma. Within a few months they had built their own counterpart to Turing's "computer," a machine known as "Madame X." From then onwards, for some ten months before the Pearl Harbor attack brought the United States into the war, there was increasing cooperation between Washington and Bletchley in what was virtually a worldwide organization for radio interception and deciphering.

Although Friedman's breakdown had prevented him from taking part in the first crucial stage of cooperation with the British, he played a key role in its development during the next four years. However, his part was civilian after a curious series of events which have never been satisfactorily explained.

Friedman left the Walter Reed Hospital on March 22 and on April 1 was returned to full-time duty. Less than three weeks later he received a letter from the Adjutant General stating that he was being "honourably discharged by reason of physical disqualification." The letter was a shock since the medical board at the hospital had recommended his return to duty; and, perhaps more important, he had not appeared before a retiring board in accordance with army regulations. Friedman protested. His protest was brushed aside. And he then returned to his former work which he was to continue, as a civilian, throughout the war.

This unusual situation was further obfuscated when, some five years later, he received a letter from the Adjutant General admitting that he had been retired without the benefit of appearing before a board. Would he care to have the 1941 hospital record reexamined?

Friedman returned to the Walter Reed Hospital for a week. "After exhaustive examinations and tests," he later wrote, "the medical officers convened to make findings in the case reported that the diagnosis of my case in 1941 was 'anxiety reaction (recovered on remission) . . . manifested by tension, insomnia . . . marked stress due to prolonged overwork on a top secret project. . . . Incapacity none. . . . The medical officers are of the opinion that this officer is fit for full active duty." Friedman now appeared before a properly constituted retiring board. They confirmed the findings of the medical officers, and he was restored to the rank he had held in 1941.

Chapter Eight

The Fumbled Catch

A NGLO-U.S. COOPERATION in the interception and decipher-ing of messages to and from enemies and potential enemies steadily increased throughout 1941 and quickly began to show re-sults. It was of course to be expected. However numerous a coun-try's intercept stations, however well organized its intelligence and cryptographic teams, only a percentage of messages will be satis-factorily picked up and deciphered. Cryptanalysts propose and bad reception, atmospherics and the other chances of a chancy game tend to dispose. Luckily enough, much of the traffic in which the United States and Britain were interested was, in the nature of things, spread across both western and eastern hemispheres. A coded order to U-boat commanders might go both to those operat-ing in the Mediterranean and to those off America's East Coast.

160

The Japanese embassy in Berlin might be receiving from Tokyo the same instructions being sent to Washington. Thus the gaps in a message imperfectly picked up by the Americans might be filled in by a British intercept of the same message broadcast to another receiver. The two-way exchange not only helped in the production of complete and ungarbled messages in ciphers which had already been broken; in addition, by increasing the amount of material on which cryptanalysts could work, it helped in the breaking of new ciphers as these were introduced by the enemy. The work of each partner thus complemented the other, particularly as the British had by this time mastered most of the Germans' repertoire of Enigma variations and the Americans had achieved a comparable success with the Japanese ciphers.

This collaboration was to aid the British in the Battle of the Atlantic — although Friedman went on record as saying that without the work of Turing that particular battle would have been lost. It was certainly to aid the Americans during the opening stages of the war with Japan. Yet its most startling result, and one which by an ironic twist of fate may have conditioned American reflexes to the Japanese pre-Pearl Harbor warnings, was a dramatic uncovering of German plans for extending the war in Europe.

The Japanese ambassador in Berlin was Baron Oshima. Following the signing of the Tripartite Pact in September, 1940, Oshima was, to a remarkable extent, taken into the confidence of the German Foreign Ministry and of the minister himself, Joachim von Ribbentrop. The result was a regular flow of despatches from Berlin to Tokyo giving details of Germany's plans and prospects, sent in what the Japanese still considered to be the most unbreakable of all unbreakable systems, Purple.

As early as January, 1941, Friedman has recorded, the Signal Intelligence Service processed a message from Baron Oshima to Tokyo forecasting that the Germans were planning to attack Russia in July. This was followed by further warnings in March and April, and on April 30 Memorandum GZ–32, summing up recent deciphered Purple messages dealing with the subject, was issued as "Early Intentions of Germany to Attack Russia." So far so good. If the Japanese could use the Purple system to relay such sensitive information then the importance of Friedman's achievement became even greater.

Complacency with the situation was brusquely shattered within the next few days. On May 5, the following message was sent by the Japanese foreign minister, Matsuoka, to Kishsaburo Nomura, the Japanese ambassador in Washington: "According to a fairly reliable source of information it appears almost certain that the United States Government is reading your code messages. Please let me know whether you have any suspicion of the above." The same day Nomura replied to Tokyo with the statement: "For our part, the most stringent precautions are taken by all custodians of codes and ciphers, as well as of other documents. On this particular matter I have nothing in mind, but pending investigation please wire any concrete instances or details which may turn up."

The messages were, most remarkably, still being sent in Purple. This fact, together with the comment that "the most stringent precautions are taken by all custodians of codes and ciphers," suggested that Matsuoka might have been referring not to Purple but to other, less important, systems. However, it became less likely as further exchanges continued between Nomura and Tokyo throughout May. Yet to the puzzlement of the Americans, further messages were still being sent in the same, and now presumably suspect, Purple.

Thus throughout May, as the Japanese were desperately discussing whether the security of Purple had been destroyed, the Americans were quite as desperately trying to discover how the Japanese knew this, if in fact they did know it.

In Tokyo, Matsuoka and the head of the Telegraphic Section in the Foreign Office began an investigation of everyone and everything connected with high-level Japanese code-systems. They reported on May 19 to the Cabinet, and as Kido Nikki, the Lord Privy Seal, recorded in his diary, to the Emperor himself. Their report, in view of what is now known, was an astonishing one since it claimed that if any Japanese messages had been read by the Americans they must have been sent by systems other than those of the Red and Purple codes. These two, it was emphasized, were still unbroken.

In Washington the counterpart investigation went on. No statement on what it discovered has ever been made, naturally enough since the motto in such matters is apt to be "all pull together." Yet the various partial explanations which have been hinted at point to a leak to the Russians — then still the Allies of Germany — and thence through the Germans to Tokyo. Ladislas Farago, who has given one account of the pre-Pearl Harbor story in *The Broken Seal*, claims that the vital error was made by Sumner Welles, anxious to woo the Russians away from Germany's side. Welles is stated to have shown the Soviet ambassador in Washington, Constantin Oumansky, a decoded message from Oshima to Tokyo discussing Germany's plans for attack. Oumansky then faced the German ambassador in Washington with the news, he in turn warned Ribbentrop that Oshima's cables to Tokyo were being read, and Ribbentrop in his turn warned Tokyo. Although supported by little corroborating evidence, the story rings true.

Whatever the true explanation of the near-disastrous leak of Purple's solution — and the practice of all pulling together dies hard — it had two side-effects which may well have combined to alter the course of history. The American investigation had revealed a good deal of slackness in the distribution of Purple decipherments and after the near-panic of the early summer, distribution was radically cut down. In particular, Roosevelt himself no longer received verbatim transcripts, but only summaries, delivered to him by an army or navy officer. Thus the full impact of the

Purple messages intercepted as war grew nearer tended to be lost on Roosevelt himself.

Far more important was the fact that the Japanese still continued to use Purple. But Matsuoka, it was estimated in Washington, must have known that Nomura's messages had been sent in Purple and not in one of the lower-level systems. What, the Americans asked themselves, could be the motive in still using Purple? One possible answer was that the Japanese hoped that in some future crisis they could send in it deliberately misleading messages. The theory did not seem particularly likely in view of the incriminating material they continued to send by the same cipher throughout the summer and autumn. Yet it remained a possibility. It fitted in with the traditional American view of Oriental cunning. And when, throughout November and early December, Purple messages seemed to bring into focus the Japanese move towards war, it was at least a psychological factor inhibiting interpretation of the messages at their face value.

Yet throughout this period the importance of the breakthrough with Purple became increasingly clear. Relations between Japan and the United States steadily deteriorated and the question of whether there would be war between the two countries slowly changed in the minds of many experts from "whether" to "when." While the evolution was taking place, every detail of the developing Japanese attitude could be followed as the Japanese ambassador's messages were intercepted, deciphered, translated and read by the Americans.

Thus they knew, within three days of the new cabinet being formed in the summer, that in the foreign minister's view, the Tripartite Pact still served as "the key stone of Japanese national policy."

By the autumn it was obvious that events were moving towards a climax. "On November 19," says the unpublished history of the Signal Corps, "Japan sent two messages which implied that a complete breakdown in relations was impending." If a breakdown in relations with the United States, with Russia or with Britain was imminent, the history said, classified information would be included in certain programs as meteorological reports. "East wind rain" would indicate a coming rupture of relations with the United States, "North wind cloudy" with Russia, and "West wind clear" with Britain. Shortly afterwards a message was intercepted giving instructions to the Japanese diplomatic corps throughout the world to begin destroying their codes and code machines. "Intelligence officers disagreed," says the history, "on just which was the most significant intercept, but all agreed that the cumulative effect pointed to war."

By these last days of November many of the organizational problems which had previously limited the value of Purple decipherments had been removed. There were still blank areas, there were still delays, particularly in translation; but for many practical purposes the men who read the Purple intercepts were as well informed on the most intimate details of Japanese policy-making as were the members of the Japanese cabinet. Thus when the Japanese ambassador in Washington was ordered to telephone Tokyo in cases of emergency, using a primitive "telephone code," the Americans took note of the fact and were soon afterwards reading Japanese comments on "the matrimonial question" (the Japanese-American negotiations) being discussed with "Miss Umeko" (Cordell Hull) and "Miss Kimiko" (President Roosevelt). After a provocative speech by the Japanese Prime Minister, the Japanese diplomat in Washington advising the ambassador, Saburo Kurusu, held an eight-minute telephone conversation with the head of the American bureau in the Japanese Foreign Office. The Americans were reading it within minutes. Later the same day, the ambassador sent a top secret cable to the Japanese foreign minister, amplifying the telephone talk. Sent in Purple, it also was being read almost simultaneously. These ominous developments were followed by an instruction from the Japanese Prime Minister to Baron Oshima in Berlin: he was to secure an interview with both Hitler and Ribbentrop and tell them of the "extreme danger that war may suddenly break out between the Anglo-Saxon nations and Japan through some clash of arms." This, Oshima was to add, might "come more quickly than anyone dreams."

In the light of the continuous stream of warnings, the disaster of Pearl Harbor at first seems even more difficult to understand without an explanation of treachery or the "revisionist" theory that Roosevelt deliberately encouraged the Japanese into their "day of infamy." The answer to the riddle may lie in coincidence, in what Friedman later called the unfortunate series of circumstances which prevented due warning being given. There was, after all, yet another, and virtually unknown, set of circumstances which J. Edgar Hoover himself appears finally to have attributed solely to coincidence.

On November 22, as the Japanese appeared intractably set on war, there appeared on page 32 of the *New Yorker* an advertisement which was drawn to Friedman's attention years later. It read: "Achtung Warning Alerte." Below, there was the instruction: "See advertisement Page 86. Monarch Publishing Co. New York." The advertisement was completed by drawings of two dice, one black and the other white. On one, there is a clear double cross and the figure 12; on the other the figure 7 appears to be rolling into the top position. Without any further evidence it might be ingenuous to consider that the advertisement warned of a double cross on the seventh day of the twelfth month. However, there is further evidence.

The same small advertisement is repeated on many other pages, all of these referring the reader to page 86. And on page 86 there was a full-column advertisement, the wording of which read as follows: "We hope you'll never have to spend a long winter's night in an air-raid shelter, but we were just thinking . . . it's only common sense to be prepared. If you're not too busy between now and Christmas, why not sit down and plan a list of the things you'll want to have on hand. . . . Canned goods, of course, and candles, Sterno, bottled water, sugar, coffee, or tea, brandy and plenty of cigarettes, sweaters and blankets, books or magazines, vitamin capsules . . . and though, it's not time, really, to be thinking of what's fashionable, we bet that most of your friends will remember to include those intriguing dice and chips which make Chicago's favourite game THE DEADLY DOUBLE $2.50 at leading Sports Goods and Department Stores Everywhere."

Above the wording there is a drawing which shows a party playing dice in a shelter; above it searchlights sweep the sky in a pattern not unlike the Rising Sun motif on the flag of the Japanese Imperial Navy. Below the wording there appears a two-headed Prussian eagle with a shield in the center marked with a double cross.

The idea of some well-wisher curiously giving the United States a curious warning by an even more curious method is suggested by two other facts. The Monarch Publishing Company was not apparently in existence in 1939, did exist in 1941, but had apparently disappeared by the following year. And the *New Yorker* could recall only that a Caucasian had come into the office, ordered the advertisements, handed over the plates for their printing, paid cash, and left without leaving his name. Mrs. Friedman's description of a "startling and unbelievable story" on her husband's file of the incident is no exaggeration. Yet after Pearl Harbor the *New Yorker*'s publishers asked the F.B.I. to investigate. J. Edgar Hoover replied that he had already been informed of the matter, and had investigated. The advertisements, he reported, were purely coincidental and his statement seemed to put the matter at rest.

By the time they were published, signs that the Japanese were bent on war were mounting at least daily and sometimes hourly. But, while the State Department was still benefiting from Purple intercepts the Navy was having less luck. On December 1, all Japanese naval ships changed their call signals and on December 4 the Japanese Navy changed its fleet code, the result being to conceal from the Americans exactly what was happening in the huge expanses of the Pacific.

Meanwhile, Washington continued to await the Japanese reply to a note which the secretary of state had sent to Tokyo during the last days of November. At midday on Saturday December 6 naval cryptographers — who were now handling Purple messages on even dates — deciphered a warning message from the Japanese foreign ministry to the Japanese embassy in Washington: the reply to Cordell Hull would be sent shortly; it would be in fourteen parts and it would have to be presented to Hull at a date and time to be given in the fourteenth part.

The first thirteen parts of the Japanese message began to come in shortly afterwards. They reiterated Japanese claims that America was an interloper in the Far East. Roosevelt, being shown these first thirteen parts at 9:30 that night commented to Harry Hopkins, his favorite adviser, that this meant war.

Many of the officers in the Signals Intelligence Service thought the same and some slept that night in their uniforms. To Friedman, as to many others, it was almost self-evident that American armed forces throughout the world must have been specially alerted.

The fourteenth part of the Japanese message began to arrive at 5:00 A.M. on the Sunday morning and was deciphered by the Americans before it was deciphered in the Japanese embassy. It announced that Japan was breaking off relations with the United States and another message ordered the embassy to present the complete message to Cordell Hull at 1:00 P.M. Lieutenant Commander Kramer, whose duty it was to deliver the final, and clinching, part of the message to the President, confirmed that 1:00 P.M. in Washington would be dawn in Hawaii.

There would seem to have been some point in passing this ominous information on to Hawaii by the fastest possible route. This was not done. The President could have warned Pearl Harbor by direct "scrambler" telephone. But he believed that the Japanese would move first against the British in Malaysia, and no one appears to have pointed out to him that 1:00 P.M. in Washington was dawn over Pearl Harbor.

Admiral Stark could similarly have warned the navy at Pearl Harbor. But an alert — "this is a war warning" — had gone out ten days before, following the earlier, ominous, Purple intercepts, and nothing more was done.

General Marshall could also have telephoned on the scrambler to General Short in Hawaii. But this was not considered secure enough, since unscrambling by the Japanese would reveal that Purple had in fact been broken. The radio to Hawaii was badly interrupted by atmospherics that morning, so the message was sent by wire to San Francisco by commercial telegraph, relayed from there and, some seven hours later, was being delivered to General Short by a messenger boy on a motorcycle when the Japanese flew in out of the rising sun to find the U.S. Pacific fleet riding defenselessly at anchor. No barrage balloons were flying, no antiaircraft guns were manned. There had, it is true, been a radar warning from one U.S. station when the Japanese planes were still well out at sea. But the warning had been ignored on the assumption that the radar blips were caused by a squadron of U.S. bombers known to be coming from the U.S. Despite the breaking of Purple, surprise was complete and shattering.

This catastrophic series of coincidences and misjudgments seemed inexplicable to many of the men who had handed to the American authorities what must still be regarded as the most important counterintelligence weapon they had ever received. Friedman himself, hearing the news of the Pearl Harbor attack on the radio, at first found it difficult to believe. For some while, his wife recalls, he could do no more than pace back and forth across the room, muttering to himself over and over again: "But they knew, they knew, they knew."

A number of commissions and boards were subsequently set up in an attempt to discover what had led to the disaster: a commission of enquiry convened by President Roosevelt nine days later, army and navy boards appointed in 1944, further investigations under the War and Navy departments, and a congressional enquiry whose hearings fill thirty-nine thick volumes. While the war lasted, criticism was muted. After it, and particularly after the congressional hearings, the revisionists began to rewrite history. They began with events eleven months before Pearl Harbor: January, 1941, when the Purple machine that might have gone to Pearl Harbor went instead to England — merely one indication, it was alleged, of President Roosevelt's anxiety to involve the United States in Britain's war. It is certainly true that Purple decipherments reaching the naval or army authorities in Pearl Harbor were routed to them *via* Washington, and it was entirely justifiable for Admiral Kimmel to comment that he was "as entitled to receive copies of intercepted Japanese communications as the British Admiralty."

From this starting point the critics moved on to a less plausible argument to explain the inaction of Washington in the face of the ever more specific warning signs. Refusing to believe that muddle and incompetence could possibly be as great as it was, ignoring the accidents of chance and circumstance that so often govern history, they relied instead on the conspiracy theory. In this interpretation, Roosevelt had deliberately refused to take action, hoping that the Japanese would deal a blow devastating enough to bring a united nation into the war on Britain's side.

Friedman's attitude to the revisionists is simple. He did not think that they had a case, and he put the matter straightforwardly twenty years after Pearl Harbor when a young nephew wrote asking his uncle's opinion of the revisionist theory he had seen in a school textbook. According to the report of the Pearl Harbor investigation, Friedman replied, "there were no messages which can be said to have disclosed exactly *where and when* the attack would be made. Hence I do not see how President Roosevelt could have avoided the attack by advance knowledge from reading such messages. In my opinion only certain members of what may be called the Extreme Right Wing believe this fable. No reliable and reputable historians believe it. All the evidence has been studied and nothing has been withheld — and there has been turned up nothing to substantiate the tale hinted at in your history book so far as I am aware. . . ."

At first glance this suggests that the Friedman of 1961 might have forgotten the Friedman of 1941 repeatedly muttering "But they knew, they knew, they knew." However, the discrepancy is nonexistent. Not even the most virulent of the anti-Roosevelt revisionists, not even those who claimed that the "Winds Execute" message had been intercepted, deciphered, then conveniently lost, seriously claimed that the Japanese had given the time and place of the coming attack.

To this extent Friedman was denying what had never been claimed. What many did claim was that the warnings which had been intercepted, deciphered and passed on during the fortnight preceding Pearl Harbor were sufficient to alert reasonable men that an attack was coming; and that Roosevelt had deliberately sidetracked those warnings. Friedman clearly believed in the first half of the argument while considering that it would be improper for him to admit it in public. He disbelieved the second half not only because he was constitutionally a pro-Roosevelt man but because he himself had witnessed, from the inside, the long series of bunglings, coincidences and mismanagement, "the series of accidents," as he put it when giving evidence before the congressional investigation, "that contrived together to prevent due warning." To a footnote in Hanson Baldwin's *The Price of Power* which stated that the essential warnings were available but "not properly processed and analysed," Friedman added the note: "Baldwin was wrong in saying the information was not properly processed, but correct in saying it was not analysed properly."

Quite apart from this, there was the continuing mystery about the "Winds Execute" messages. Even Roberta Wohlstetter, writing in *Pearl Harbor: Warning and Decision,* the most authoritative analysis of the event, is forced to admit that "it is impossible with the evidence available to establish whether or not an authentic execute message of the winds code was received." And even the Japanese have two versions of events: that the message was sent and that it was not sent. However, two officers, one naval and one army, were later to claim that such a message had not only been sent but had been intercepted before the attack. Friedman himself did not believe that this was so, but testified to an even more remarkable state of affairs: that a message of comparable significance, received early on December 7, had not only been mistranslated but had been passed on with the omission of the vital word linking it with the United States.

Giving evidence before the congressional investigation Friedman said that Captain Safford of the navy had told him of one pre-Pearl Harbor interception. "Captain Safford," he said, "indicated that there was — there had been a 'winds execute' message; that no copies of it were to be found in the Navy files, and that nevertheless there had been testimony to the effect that it had been intercepted. His story was that it was intercepted by one of their East Coast stations, he believed, and was promptly forwarded into Washington, and I don't recall now who got it."

Safford's evidence was refuted. Nevertheless, he stuck to his story. In fact he gave it further muscle when, after the congressional hearings in 1946, he visited Friedman to watch the demonstration of a ciphering machine of interest to them both. After the demonstration, Friedman called him aside and asked him to auto-graph a copy of the evidence which he, Safford, had given before the Joint Committee.

"He did so," Friedman wrote on the back of the document,

> and after thanking him I asked him how he *now* felt about the "Winds Execute Message." He looked at me rather intently for a few seconds and then said: "I feel I didn't *prove* it existed." He went on to elaborate on this a bit and then told me that he himself had prepared a "war warn-ing" message of his own, to send in case higher authorities weren't going to do something like that. I said: "But it *might* have been based on an erroneous or false 'Winds Execute,'" whereupon he countered with this: "When you're going to by-pass higher authority be d— sure your facts are right." He went on to say that not only did he prepare such a warning message but he also had it encoded — and that the man who encoded it *remembered* the fact and the message. I asked S whether this was introduced in evidence and he said it had not. Why? The man who encoded it was out of the country and not available until after the Congressional Investigation had been completed, so [he] didn't deem it wise to bring up the matter, since he could produce no corroborating witness.

Here Friedman interpolated the following note: "I guess S meant by this statement that he had no opportunity with that man as to his recollection, *before* testifying that he had prepared a warning message and had it encoded."

Friedman's note then continued

> "In case the subject is reopened, I know I can get him to tell his story," Safford said. It is clear that S still is of firm conviction there was an authentic "Winds Execute," that it was intercepted, deciphered, passed around and has disappeared.

I neglected to say above that Safford didn't send the warning message he had prepared — because he understood that McCullom's message was being sent. He saw McC's message and was satisfied with it, so saw no need to send his own. He learned only long afterwards that McC's message had *never* been sent.

On the card in the Friedman archives attached to the document there is a note by Mrs. Friedman. "W.F.F.," it says, "*never* supported Captain Safford in any of the latter's statements concerning this autographed message." This is no doubt true. But there is one point quite as important as Friedman's belief that no "Winds Execute" was ever received, and that is Safford's honest belief that one had been intercepted. Friedman's statement that "It is clear that S still is of firm conviction there was an authentic 'Winds Execute,' that it was intercepted, decoded, passed around — and has disappeared," should effectively remove any shred of belief that Safford was muddling the story for his own purposes, personal or political.

Human fallibility being what it is, Safford's story could, without supporting evidence, easily be written off entirely. But there is supporting evidence. It came from Colonel Sadtler, head of the army's communication service at the time of Pearl Harbor, and while it was subsequently altered, it is sufficiently in line with Safford's to be mildly disturbing.

"He [Colonel Sadtler] indicated," Friedman told the congressional investigation, "that the 'Winds Execute' message had come in on the — some time on the fourth or fifth of December. I don't think he was clear himself as to which of those two days it was. ... There was apparently nothing to substantiate the existence of the message. Then, if I remember correctly, I asked Colonel Sadtler whether he had a copy, had ever gotten or seen a copy of this message, and his answer was, if I remember correctly, that he himself hadn't seen a copy, but that he had been told by somebody that the copies had been ordered or directed to be destroyed by General Marshall. Of course, I regarded this as merely hearsay evidence and nothing more than that; highly inconceivable that such a thing would happen. And when I talked over the Pearl Harbor story with Captain Safford, I probably just passed that out as one of those crazy things that get started. I shouldn't have done it. I certainly had no idea that he would repeat it."

Friedman was no doubt right to kill the suggestion about Marshall. But if this was a detail of Sadtler's story embroidered on for reasons political or otherwise, the story itself has more substance than Friedman's account to the investigating committee would suggest. Once again, the unpublished Signals history casts a fresh light on what happened, giving details of Sadtler's call from the navy that "the message is in" or words to that effect. When Sadtler passed this on there was the suggestion that it might be a false alarm. It appeared to him that no special action was going to be taken and he returned to his office very much disturbed. "To him," the record continues, "the winds execute message meant war, and he had no doubt that this was indeed an execute message. The more he thought about it, the greater concern he felt. Sitting down at his typewriter, he typed out the draft of a message he intended to recommend be sent to the overseas commanders in the Philippine Islands, Hawaii, and Panama. As Sadtler remembered the message, it read: 'Reliable information indicated war with Japan very near future. Take every precaution to prevent repetition of Port Arthur. Notify the Navy. Marshall.' "

However, when he proposed that the warning be sent, he was told that the commanders in the areas concerned already had ample notification. The matter was dropped.

"Still dissatisfied, Colonel Sadtler made one more attempt," the Signals history continues. "He went to see the secretary of the General Staff, Lt. Col. Walter B. Smith who he knew would have direct access to General Marshall, and again told his story. Smith asked Sadtler what he had done, and upon learning that Sadtler had already talked to G-2 and to War Plans, Smith said he did not wish to discuss it further. Sadtler did not show his proposed warning message to either Gerow or Smith. Unfortunately, the message was lost. Colonel Sadtler later checked with members of his office staff; none had any recollection of the message or, indeed, of his having written it. Colonel Sadtler typed the message himself, made no copy, and did not know what became of it, although he had intended to keep it."

As with Safford, there is the remembered message and the later failure to find any trace of it. Either of two conclusions can be drawn. One, held by the revisionists, is that the messages were conveniently "lost" for political purposes. The other, held by Friedman, is that the messages never existed and that both Safford and Sadtler were, either innocently or for reasons of their own, remembering with advantages.

Yet it seems at least possible that the mystery has a more ordinary explanation which would account for Friedman's persistent rejection of the conspiracy theory and also for the various qualifications with which he habitually hedged any comments on the Pearl Harbor imbroglio. The explanation is that both men genuinely believed that a Winds Execute order had been issued — whether or not they were correct is comparatively irrelevant — and that their pleas for action were lost in the fog of incompetence and bad luck which seems to have enveloped the service authorities in Washington throughout the weeks leading up to Pearl Harbor.

This is made even more likely by the extraordinary story told by Friedman shortly after he had recorded the accounts given by Safford and Sadtler. A few days after Pearl Harbor, he said, he had seen a message issued from Tokyo on December 7 and translated by the army as: "Relations between Japan and England are not in accordance with expectations."

"Although I was ill, I saw clearly enough that the message on its face was absurd," he continued. "Any fool would realise that on December seventh Tokio was not going to send any message out saying 'Relations between Japan and England are not in accordance with expectations' when the die had already been cast, and I came to the tentative conclusion that there was something wrong with that message."

Friedman asked for a retranslation and discovered what he described as "a very surprising situation." The code-word *hattori* which had been translated to give "relations between Japan and — are not in accordance with expectations" should have given "relations between Japan and — are on the brink of catastrophe."

"Moreover," Friedman went on, "I found that the message of December 7, 1941, which mentions only relations between Japan and England, had another defect in that the original intercept included the word 'minami,' meaning the U.S.A., as well as the word 'koyanagi,' meaning England. That double error produced a concatenation of circumstances that I thought later was just an additional one in the series of accidents that contrived together to prevent due warning, because had that originally been translated accurately 'on the brink of catastrophe,' 'on the verge of disaster,' and so on, had that come in, it would have got immediate attention. The same thing would have happened had the translation mentioned the United States."

Pressure of work on cryptographers and translators, the lack of effective machinery which would sort the really significant messages from the scores of others, and of any system of analysis which would have enabled Intelligence to do its job, combined with bad luck and bad judgment to produce the disaster of Pearl Harbor. There was no need for conspiracy; how well this was appreciated at the highest levels in Washington is not known. Perhaps the influence of America's near-Allies was greater than either knew and the United States felt confident that, like the British, they could muddle through to winning the last battle.

Chapter Nine

Pearl Harbor to Peace

A MERICA'S ENTRY into the war in December, 1941, helped to regularize and make easier the cryptographic collaboration with the British which had been fostered by Friedman, and his navy counterparts, for roughly a year.

It also regularized the work on which Mrs. Friedman had been occupied for some weeks before Pearl Harbor. Her task was the establishment of a cryptographic organization for what was to become General William Donovan's Office of Strategic Services. The operation had begun on November 10 — while America was still at peace — when she had been asked to prepare code and cipher material for what was still Donovan's Office of the Coordination of Information. For three weeks she and her staff at Coast Guard headquarters had laid the lines for cryptographic links between Washington and Donovan's London office. It had been planned that two small Hagelin machines would be used, but these failed to arrive as expected and one of Mrs. Friedman's *coups* was to obtain for Donovan's use two machines which had been earmarked for other departments.

On December 2 she moved into the Donovan organization and for the rest of the month she and her staff prepared special keys, alphabet strips and other devices for use in the field. "This class of material was devised and prepared," she later reported to Donovan, "for the especial and particular use of your organisation alone and exists nowhere else." In addition, she began to recruit cryptographers for the organization and to lay down ground rules for the training in code and cipher use which had to be given to Donovan's men going on secret operations. She was also prescient enough to suggest something that had apparently escaped everyone else. "I should like to recommend," she wrote, "that a specially prepared oath be taken by all persons in your organisation, including Civil Service employees and all others without distinction. I prepared a special oath applicable to the message center, and all persons employed therein so far have executed this oath. An oath suitable for the general personnel could be devised and prepared by the Personnel Office, and executed in each case as the person reports for duty."

Elizebeth Friedman's work was now quite as secret as that of her husband. That did not prevent Friedman himself from being called before the director of Military Intelligence on one occasion and being severely reprimanded on suspicion that he had "talked shop" with his wife. The allegation was untrue, since both husband and wife observed a Trappist silence about their professional work, but it is typical of the distrust, at times verging on paranoia, with which some service officers regarded the cryptographers. "I was so completely taken not only aback," Friedman wrote later, "but also with surprise and by the vehemence of the Major-General's attack on me that I lost my tongue completely, and failed to ask for permission to sleep in the same room and/or bed with my wife."

While Elizebeth Friedman was helping to lay the groundwork for what was to become one of the most famous of all wartime undercover organizations, her husband was once again sidetracked from purely cryptographic work into supervision of a rapidly growing department. He had for long encouraged collaboration between army and navy cryptographic services and the process culminated in the summer of 1942 when the navy handed over their Purple machine to the army, together with their files of intercepts in the Purple code. From then onwards the army was responsible for the interception, deciphering, and distribution of all Japanese diplomatic messages.

A massive expansion of activities and a huge increase in staff were involved in the transition. Friedman's small handful of men, which had grown to an only slightly larger handful by the outbreak of the European war in 1939, had become more than three hundred by the time of Pearl Harbor and more than a dozen I.B.M. machines were soon in use. However, this was only a faint shadow of the more than 10,000 men and women who in 1945 were working in what had become first the Signal Security Service and then the Signal Security Agency.

The Munitions Building had quickly become too small to hold the organization and in the summer of 1942 Friedman and his unit moved to Arlington Hall, a former girls' school three miles out of Washington across the Potomac. Here, too, an overflow area was soon required, and before the end of the year, the bulk of training had been shifted to Vint Hill Farms in the foothills of the Blue Ridge Mountains fifty miles from Washington.

Friedman had by this time recovered from the worst of the collapse which had taken him to the hospital early in 1941. But his brief "although I was ill," when recalling for the Pearl Harbor hearings the events of December, 1941, conceals the fact that he was, by then, once more having psychiatric treatment. Depression was again the main trouble and an old friend has recalled how on one occasion he saw Friedman about to drive off in his car with a coil of rope on the back seat. The obvious question brought a surprising answer: "I'm looking for a tree to hang myself." The answer was probably perverse rather than explanatory. Nevertheless, despite improvement, collapse was still a specter lurking in the background.

None who worked with Friedman knew more than that he was under strain and overworked. He kept his image, as he kept it throughout the worst that was to come, successfully presenting to colleagues and friends the picture of a man successfully in control of his task, his mind and his future.

In Arlington Hall he seemed to be at the height of his powers: trim, cool, and justifiably confident of his own ability. Here he sat a few feet away from his technical assistant Lambros Callimahos, to whom he would pass a constant stream of brief notes about the technical papers arriving on his desk. "He was meticulous in his habits, whether on staff policy papers or in technical exposition," Callimahos has said. "He was a stickler for precise and accurate terminology, and he coined many of the words used today in our profession, beginning with the term 'cryptanalysis.' He would first think out the problem or situation in broad outlines, and then would map out points a, b, c . . . in logical progression, with utmost clarity of exposition and the greatest attention to detail. He wasted but little time or motion, and especially on technical matters he knew instinctively when he was on the wrong track — a splendid attribute for any cryptanalyst."

After Japan's entry into the war the importance of Friedman's breaking of Purple quickly increased. Baron Oshima's meetings in Berlin with German Foreign Office officials became more frequent. These were now meetings between Allies, and the baron's diplomatic reports, often being studied by the Americans as they were being read in Tokyo, usefully complemented the German Wehr-macht and Luftwaffe messages read by the British through their decipherments of Enigma.

Soon, Japanese plans for South America were also being revealed through the broken diplomatic code. Even before the end of December, 1941, General Marshall was informing the under secretary of state, Mr. Sumner Welles, of the Japanese intentions, disclosed by intercepts of messages in Purple, to wreck the coming Rio Conference and the Good Neighbor Policy which it was hoped would increase support for the Allies in South America. A note dated December 31 was accompanied by a long list of summaries covering messages from the Japanese Foreign Office and its officials in Buenos Aires, and even warned of the specific tasks given to certain diplomats.

South America had become important as a source of information for the well-organized Axis network watching shipping movements between the United States and Britain, and here the cryptographic work of the previous few years began to pay dividends. Shortly before midnight on March 12, 1942, for instance, the radio monitor station at Laredo, Texas, intercepted a long coded call from Rio de Janeiro which began VVVV EVI EVI EVI. It was known from internal evidence that the message came from a member of a group which based both its calls and its transposition cipher on the Alba-tross edition of Axel Munthe's *The Story of San Michele,* an edition excluded by copyright arrangements from the United States and Britain. A different page of the book was used each day, the page being determined by adding, to a constant number assigned to each agent, the number of the month and the number of the day of the month on which the call was sent out. When these three numbers were added up they gave the number of the designated page. The last three letters of the last line on this designated page, reversed, gave the call sign for the sending station on that particular day. It was known that the number assigned to the Rio operator was 56

he Arlington Hall group, c. 1943. Seated left to right are Colonel Harald
. Hayes, Colonel W. Preston Corderman, William Friedman. Standing
ft to right, Colonel Johnston, Lieutenant Colonel Jones, Colonel Stark,
ieutenant Colonel Molstead.

and by adding to this 3 for March and 12 for the day of the third month, a total of 71 was obtained. Turning to page 71 it was found that the last word on the page was "give" — which, reversed, gave the expected EVI.

Without much difficulty the message was then decoded: TEXT SIXTY FROM VESTA TO SETIN. QUEEN MARY REPORTED OFF RECIFE BY STEAMSHIP CAMPEIRO ON ELEVENTH AT EIGHTEEN O'CLOCK MIDDLE EUROPEAN TIME. Further messages were duly intercepted and the *Queen Mary* told that the enemy knew of her movements.

Much information about Axis agents in South America followed the breaking of the main German diplomatic code, a feat which sprang directly from Anglo-U.S. cooperation. The United States intercept station on Hawaii had been picking up messages in this code before the outbreak of the European war, but Friedman's cryptographic team had failed to get very far in breaking it. The British had had even less success; for a while they had even given up intercepting such messages, considering it a waste of effort.

However, interchange was interchange, and in the summer of 1941 the British passed over to the Americans twenty-five lines of intercepted material sent out in this code. At first the intercepts meant very little. Then the German operator at a station in South America made a mistake; or, more accurately, he was lazy in enciphering a particularly long message. Moreover, by the same kind of chance which had given the Allies a key to the ADFGVX code in 1918, the long and complete message was picked up by one of the American intercept stations. The laziness in enciphering plus the twenty-five lines passed over by the British, enabled Kullback's team in Washington ultimately, with considerable effort, to break the code.

German confidence that it was still absolutely secure was shown in a message from Buenos Aires shortly afterwards. Asked by Berlin for confirmation of its physical safety, the Argentine embassy sent a reply intended to be reassuring. The room where encoding took place, it reported, could only be approached through one door. Outside the door there always stood an armed guard, accompanied by an Alsatian dog. The encoder, moreover, always worked with a loaded revolver on the table beside him. Therefore, it was added, there could be no chance whatever of the code being secured by Allied agents. The possibility that it might be broken was not even mentioned.

As Anglo-U.S. collaboration increased, a number of interchange visits were arranged, a fore-runner of the postwar arrangements by which Americans are posted, on rota, to the British cryptographic headquarters in Cheltenham and British cryptographers are stationed in Washington. Among the first to visit Friedman was Oliver Strachey, brother of Lytton Strachey, the writer, and a pillar of the British cryptographic establishment. Strachey had been persuaded into the Foreign Office in 1914 at the age of forty because of his cryptographic ability, previously exercised purely as an amateur; "and there," in the words of his *Times* obituarist in 1960, "happily and most usefully, he remained until his retirement."

Between the two world wars Strachey had written a number of publications for the War Office, all highly technical, all highly secret, and at least one being printed in an edition of less than a hundred copies. Now Strachey met the author of *The Index of Coincidence,* to the great enjoyment of both.

There was also a visit by Friedman to Bletchley, where for some weeks he discussed not only the latest cryptographic problems but the measures needed to conceal from the enemy just how successful the Allies had already been.

While Friedman was thus acting as liaison officer between the American and British efforts, his wife was almost continuously involved in a succession of cryptographic activities at the Treasury. Much of this concerned the interception and deciphering of messages from German agents or sympathizers in South America, many of which dealt with Allied shipping movements. At times, to Elizebeth Friedman's dismay, the government's left hand ignored what its right hand was doing, a classic example being the *Annual Report of the Emergency Advisory Committee for Political Defense* published in 1943. She had only unwillingly furnished the committee with details of a number of systems and encipherments being used by German agents in South America. These certainly revealed the political involvement of various ostensibly neutral countries, but if any hint of the Treasury successes were made public the result could be disastrous. The 1943 report not only hinted at the successes; it published verbatim notes of actual messages sent by one particular station, thus effectively warning the enemy to switch station, ciphers and wavelengths.

Elizebeth also became involved in the case of the doll woman, Velvalee Dickinson. In August, 1942, the F.B.I. asked the censors to watch for references to dolls in letters being sent abroad from the United States. Just what had suggested the idea that dolls might be used as a cover for messages is not known, but shortly afterwards the authorities arrested, in Manhattan, an importer of expensive dolls which she sold at a shop on Madison Avenue. What had aroused the censor's suspicion was the curious wording of the numerous letters which the importer sent to an assortment of correspondents in South America. Mrs. Friedman was consulted when the government was preparing its case. She refused to give evidence in court since the letters had, she decided, been written in open code, that is, a code language which was an individual thing, whose meaning might vary slightly from letter to letter, and about which it would be impossible to give conclusive evidence. What she did do, was to suggest a plausible meaning for many of the apparently harmless keywords in the letters. "My family," she proposed, meant "the Japanese fleet" or "a group of agents." "Three English dolls" could be English warships of three different classes, such as battleship, cruiser, destroyer: "torn in middle" could mean "torpedoed amidships"; "no longer in shops," could be interpreted as "many ships earlier in port have now gone out into action." It had earlier seemed likely that the writer was especially interested in naval affairs and Elizebeth Friedman was convinced that not only did the nationality of the dolls mentioned mean ships from different navies, but that a check on the ships in ports from which letters had been posted would provide at least circumstantial evidence.

Her suggestions were followed up, most effectively. In 1944 the famous doll woman was found guilty of sending out naval intelligence to the Japanese via South America, fined 10,000 dollars, and sent to prison for ten years.

The case of the doll woman, ending with prosecution in open court, was one in which American success, if not in code breaking at least in something very like it, could not be concealed. In the wider field concealment of success had always been a major problem. Yardley's book on the American Black Chamber was only the most blatantly obvious example of the revelation that could cause the immediate shutting-off of information. The wartime problem can be stated simply enough: if the breaking of an enemy code or cipher has given specific information, how is it possible to take action on that information without giving the game away?

An early example had come before America entered the war but after Britain had started her blockade of Europe. Interception and decipherment of German messages from South America by Friedman's team revealed that an important load of skillfully concealed platinum would soon be on its way to Italy. But it would almost certainly be checked by the British at Gibraltar who were given precise details of what contraband was being carried, and where. Yet to impound the vessel would probably disclose the fact that an important German code had been broken.

Forewarned, the British were able to solve the problem. An apparently fortuitous series of "chances" led to one particular part of the cargo being carefully inspected, and an "accident" led to the discovery of the contraband load. The Germans continued to use the same code.

One early example of the need to disguise the success achieved by the Americans in breaking enemy code and cipher systems arose not with Purple but with one of the Japanese naval codes broken by naval cryptologists. This followed the spectacular American success in the battle of Midway, later recognized as the turning point of the war in the Pacific, and a battle where victory was directly the result of cryptographic success.

On May 5, 1942, Imperial General Headquarters in Tokyo issued an order for a combined army and navy invasion of strategic points in the Aleutian Islands and of Midway. More than two hundred vessels would assemble in Hiroshima Bay and then, over four days, move out in five main forces. They would occupy the strategic bases from which Japan would be able to mount a permanent protective air screen covering the approaches to her earlier conquests.

The order should have been issued in a new version of the Japanese naval code which, the Americans knew from their radio intercepts, was to have been introduced on April 1. But the new code-books had not been issued in time and the date for their use had been put on, first to May 1, then to June 1 — one of the most fateful delays in the whole of the Pacific war. The existing code had been solved by the Americans to the extent that some 90 percent of messages sent in it, or parts of messages, could be read, and it was clear from the intercepted order that a massive invasion force would soon be at sea. But, maddeningly, two vital facts, the date of invasion and the exact place still remained concealed by the code. Midway was of course one candidate for place; but so was Oahu in Hawaii and so was Dutch Harbour in the Aleutians. For Admiral Nimitz, with barely sufficient ships to protect any one target, let alone all three, a wrong guess would be disastrous.

Then, on May 20, a second order was issued from Tokyo. It spelled out the tactics to be used and suggested that the target of the main invasion force was being given by the Japanese as the map symbol AF. It might be Midway.

The cryptanalysts now cabled to American Headquarters on Midway telling them to send a message in plaintext reporting that the fresh-water distillation plant on the island had broken down. The ruse worked. Two days later the Japanese, having intercepted the message in plaintext, radioed in code to headquarters that "AF" would soon be short of fresh water.

That fixed the place. The time was still missing and only after two more days' wrestling with the Japanese date code was the answer given: June 3.

On June 1, the new code went into operation and the American cryptographers found themselves faced with a mass of indecipherable messages. But this was no longer so important. By the time the Japanese invasion fleet was approaching Midway the three American carriers *Enterprise, Hornet* and *Yorktown* were waiting on the flanks.

In the battle that followed American carrier-based planes sank four enemy carriers for the loss of the *Yorktown*. For all practical purposes, the Japanese had lost their seaborne air arm. Their westward expansion across the Pacific had been halted in its tracks.

The naval authorities had done everything possible to spread the story that Japan's invasion fleet had been discovered by chance. It seemed likely that they had succeeded. Then, while the battered Japanese fleet was still withdrawing, the *Chicago Tribune* published a sensational story headed "Navy Had Word of Jap Plan to Strike at Sea." The paper made no mention of codes or ciphers but gave such a detailed account of American knowledge before the battle that a shock wave of anger rolled through the Navy Department. Surely the Japanese would draw their own conclusions from this revelation.

The Japanese did, in fact, alter their naval code again soon afterwards and many outside naval intelligence circles assumed that the *Chicago Tribune* was responsible. "I was among those who believed the assumption to be true," Friedman himself wrote years later. "Navy COMINT security was extremely tight. It was several years later that I learned at first hand that the assumption was erroneous — the Japanese made their usual, *regular* and periodic change on schedule and the Tribune disclosures apparently did not have the effect of triggering off the change."

Despite this, the navy called a grand jury investigation but finally agreed that it should be called off in the interests of secrecy. Then, when the whole thing appeared to have been forgotten, a U.S. Representative rose in the House and made a speech castigating the *Chicago Tribune* for publishing its story. "American boys will die because of the article," he accused before going on to say that "somehow our Navy had secured and broken the secret code of the Japanese navy." In the words of the *American Legion Magazine,* "Navy officials, after they recovered from apoplectic fits, held their breath again. And again Japan either missed the item or simply failed to believe it."

The need to conceal that a code or cipher had been broken sometimes made it doubtful whether information obtained through it should be acted upon at all. The most famous example came in April, 1943, when Admiral Yamamoto, the commander in chief of the Combined Japanese Fleet, decided to make a five-day tour of Pacific bases. His itinerary was sent to each base he was to visit; it was sent in considerable detail and in a code which American cryptographers had already broken. The result was that some days before the tour was to be made the times of Yamamoto's arrival and departure on every leg of his journey were known to the Americans. Just as important, his route brought him within range of American planes and he was known to be almost paranoically punctual.

The American commanders were now faced with an awkward decision. If Yamamoto were successfully shot down there was little chance of his being superseded by a more efficient commander. But an interception of the kind planned could hardly be by chance and must surely reveal that the Japanese code had been broken. But it was decided to take that chance. And in case the Japanese did suspect, there was a "cover" to hand. There were known to be friendly agents still operating in some of the areas which the admiral would be visiting. Information was still being radioed in to the Australian coast-watchers and they in turn passed it on to the American authorities. If necessary, this could be leaked back to the Japanese as the source which had been acted on.

On the morning of April 18, eighteen P-38's took off for a 400-odd mile flight at wave-top height. Little more than two hours later they arrived off Bougainville — just as the tiny specks of Yamamoto's plane and escort appeared in the distance. A few minutes later, the admiral's aircraft was sent blazing into the Bougainville jungle. The Americans returned with the loss of a single plane.

The facts of Yamamoto's death are openly on record. But there is another incident in which, it has been claimed, the need to preserve a broken code's apparent security brought about a famous death, that of the film actor, Leslie Howard, whose plane was shot down by the Germans in June, 1943, while being flown from Lisbon to London. There were later rumors that the Germans had expected Churchill to be on board, and in *The Hinge of Fate* Churchill speculated that this might have been so. The Air Ministry, curiously enough, claimed to have thought otherwise, issuing a statement which said in part: "There is no evidence to suggest that the crews [of the German planes] had orders to attack this particular aircraft." Little more was heard of the story until after publication of *The Ultra Secret* in 1975. Reviewing it, an American commentator came flatly out with the statement that there had been warning of the coming attack on Howard's plane, but that any alteration of plan would have revealed that the German messages were being read.

Commentators can make mistakes. But the incident was, it appears, discussed quite openly at a meeting of O.S.S. veterans in Washington. Old men can certainly remember not only with advantages but out of focus, and not too much should be made of after-dinner reminiscences. However, one of the veterans, asked to remember more, would merely say that it had been a British affair and that any details he knew personally had been read in *The Ultra Secret.* But Howard's name is not even mentioned in *The Ultra Secret* and the riddle remains.

The main threat to the security of the Purple breakthrough came in the autum of 1944 when, after the invasion of Europe, it was becoming more and more useful as a source of German plans. The full use then made of it has so far not been admitted either by the British or by the Americans, neither being anxious to reveal exactly what intelligence information came from code breaking and what came from sources within the German armed forces, or from the German cryptographic services.

Nevertheless, even before D-Day in June, 1944, repercussions of the decipherment of Purple were making themselves felt at General Eisenhower's headquarters in southern England. On one occasion the Japanese military attaché in Berlin was given a detailed tour of the German West Wall, the huge defensive system built along the Channel coast. Back in the German capital the attaché wrote for the military in Tokyo a 1000-word report of what he had seen. It was enciphered in Purple and radioed to Japan. Luckily, reception was good, in London as well as in Tokyo, and Eisenhower's staff was reading the plaintext as soon as the Japanese.

However, in the autumn of 1944 it became known that Governor Dewey of New York, campaigning against Roosevelt in the presidential election, was threatening to raise the specter of the Pearl

Harbor disaster. He was planning, it was learned, not merely to repeat the criticisms of presidential slackness which had already been bitterly made against Roosevelt, but to support them with the apparently damning revelation that long before the Japanese attack the Americans had been following each Japanese diplomatic move by reading the most secret instructions from Tokyo. How in these circumstances, he would ask, had the Pearl Harbor disaster been possible?

How much Roosevelt knew of Dewey's plans is not known. But one man who did know was General Marshall. Taking matters into his own firm hands he wrote a brief account of what the breaking of Purple meant to the conduct of the war and implored Dewey to make no mention of the success. He prefaced his appeal with a note which asked Dewey to do one of two things: either pledge himself to "not communicating [the letter's] contents to any other person" and then read on; or return the letter unread. Dewey returned the letter unread, with the brief comment that it could only have been sent by an officer in Marshall's position with the knowledge of the President.

Marshall refused to give up. By return he wrote another, and longer, letter. In this he stated that neither the Secretary of State for War nor the President had any idea that the letter was being sent or even prepared. It had been written entirely on his own initiative "because the military hazards involved are so serious that I feel some action is necessary to protect the interests of our armed forces."

Marshall went on to explain how if the Japanese codes had not been broken the American forces at Midway would "almost certainly have been some 3,000 miles out of place," and how details of Japanese garrisons, fleet movements and convoys were known on a day-to-day basis. However, that was not all.

As far as the European war was concerned, it was true that they had broken other codes. Nevertheless, "our main basis of informa-

Friedman receiving Exceptional Civilian Service Award, 1944.

tion regarding Hitler's intentions in Europe is obtained from Baron Oshima's messages from Berlin reporting his interviews with Hitler and other officials to the Japanese Government. . . . The conduct of General Eisenhower's campaign and of all operations in the Pacific are closely related in conception and timing to the information we secretly obtain through these intercepted codes. They contribute greatly to the victory and tremendously to the saving in American lives, both in the conduct of current operations and in looking towards the early termination of the war." Dewey kept silent.

It is typical of Friedman that years later, when the contents of Marshall's letter became known, he should try to discover what help Marshall had had in writing it. The reason, he explained, was that it "gave a misimpression as to who deserved credit for getting Midway information; that credit belongs to the Navy." His informant said "yes — but there were things about that which came from the Army too." In spite of Friedman's punctilious concern that the navy should get its due, Marshall's office was right: by 1942 the efforts of the army and navy cryptographers had become so complementary that for many practical purposes they had become merged into one. Both, moreover, had eventually had a hand in perfecting Sigaba, one of the most effective and efficient machines in whose design Friedman had played a major part. The basic design of the Sigaba was the army's, and Friedman himself held patents on many of the features it incorporated.

Although the machine's value was admitted even before the outbreak of war, money for its production was not available, and it was largely through Friedman's friendship with Admiral Wenger that the navy was induced to finance its production. Navy cryptographers also contributed their own ideas of how it could be improved but both the original model and the new models which became available as the war progressed, were basically the result of Friedman's work.

The outcome was a machine produced in quantity by the Teletype Corporation in Chicago, known as ECM Mark II in the navy and as Sigaba by the army. It was large, making up three separate 300-pound loads, consumed much electricity, and could be moved only by truck. It was used in all theaters of operations at highest levels of command, and even by President Roosevelt in Washington. So great was the importance attached to it that none of America's allies was allowed even to see it, let alone have it, not even the British, who operated their own electric cipher machine known as Typex. However, in order to ease communications between U.S. and British forces, adapters were developed so that messages could be sent in cipher between Sigaba and Typex units. That was all. If top cryptographic priority lay in preventing the Japanese from discovering that Purple had been broken, the need to keep Sigaba secure ran it a close second.

The machine did, however, have one built-in risk which Friedman admitted when interviewed for the official Signal history after the war. "The on-line features had a serious security disadvantage," says the history, "in that the operator on the transmitting end sometimes forgot — when passing from unclassified traffic sent in the clear to classified — to flip the switch that would connect the on-line crypto equipment. At least twice this happened during the war. One message gave the travel route of General MacArthur during the New Guinea campaign. The clear text, if intercepted, would have given the enemy a prize opportunity. Frantic corrections were made to cover up the error, without MacArthur's ever knowing what happened. To prevent such errors, S.I.S. later required that a monitor be assigned each channel, his full task being to listen and make sure that when classified traffic was being sent the on-line cipher machine was switched on."

Late in the autumn of 1944 Friedman had a bad, but only momentary shock when told that the Japanese had captured Sigaba in New Guinea. With relief he found that Sigaba, quite apart from being his own particular brainchild, was also the name of a small village.

The real trouble began the following February when American forces, having beaten back the last German offensive in the Battle of the Bulge, were again advancing towards the German frontier. On February 3, they occupied the French city of Colmar, only twelve miles from the Rhine. That evening a truck carrying the three units comprising a Sigaba machine was parked in the main square of Colmar. The following morning the truck, and its load, had disappeared.

This would have been serious even in different circumstances. But the front line was less than twelve miles away. Daring German commandos had earlier rescued Mussolini from an apparently impregnable mountaintop stronghold and it was not inconceivable that they had spirited away a working specimen of America's most secret cipher machine.

When Washington heard the news, the first reaction was to suspend all enciphering by Sigaba until a new set of keys could be used. It is true that even if the machine was by some feat now in German hands, the enemy would be able to read its messages only after they had discovered which particular keys were being used for encipherment. That, however, was only one part of the story. Once German cryptographers had studied the machine, then taken it apart, the methods of encipherment would be exposed and the chances of breaking all messages sent by it greatly increased.

In Washington a number of awful possibilities were considered. If the Sigaba machine was in German hands the danger was not only that Allied messages could be deciphered but that the Germans might be able to duplicate the machine and thus give their own messages much of the security which had so far been an American prerogative. Another possibility was that the French intelligence service, very active in that part of France, might have decided to remove the Sigaba and then, having learned how to copy it, return it with the apologetic plea of a mistake.

During the following February days an extraordinary series of special efforts were made to find the missing truck. Every American and French unit commander in Sixth Army Group was ordered to compare *personally* the serial number of each of his vehicles with that of the missing vehicle. Special roadblocks were set up throughout the area to check every vehicle passing through them and special low reconnaissance sorties were flown by L-5 liaison planes in the hope of locating an abandoned truck. All efforts drew a blank, as did espionage attempts to sense anything on the German side that would betray an unexpected success.

It was in March that two of the loads were found on the banks of a small stream near the town of Selestat, a few miles from Colmar. Only after the damming and dredging of the stream did the third one come to light. But how long had they been there? It was forty-five days since they had been taken, ample time for inspection of the contents and the smuggling of sketches through the Allied lines.

Eventually, it was established that the loads had not been inspected. On the night of February third, it was finally discovered, a French driver had lost his truck in Colmar and "liberated" an American vehicle he found momentarily unguarded. Fearful of being charged with stealing the loads, he had pushed them from the truck at the first convenient place.

Even in the final stages of the war, the value of Purple messages remained. Indeed, as the territory between the advancing Anglo-U.S. armies in the west and the advancing Russians in the east continued to diminish, these messages had an additional use: they enabled General Marshall to pass on to the Russians detailed information on current German intentions as the Third Reich began to disintegrate.

Thus in April, 1945, he sent to the U.S. Military Mission in Moscow, for transmission to the Russians, a report of Hitler's plans as given a few days earlier to Baron Oshima in Berlin. On the fourth the German undersecretary for foreign affairs, Von Steengracht, had reported to him: "As a result of the Russian advance to the Vienna Region we Germans are giving up the greater part of Croatia and falling back on a line including Zagreb. Depending on the future war situation we may be forced to fall back again to German territory and in that case the line in Italy will necessarily have to be pulled back to the frontier area."

The report went on to give the news, vitally important for the Allied armies in the west, that the Germans still believed it possible for their forces in the Ruhr encirclement to fight their way out, and went on: "The shattering of the Rhine line was completely beyond German expectations and it cannot fail to have an effect on the offensive which Germany has planned for the Eastern Front."

On the fifth, Oshima saw Von Ribbentrop, who gave him more details of the situation, all of which were sent without delay to Japan, and were being read in Washington by the time they were being deciphered in Tokyo. And the following day, Oshima was given one more crucial piece of news from Ribbentrop: "Although it has been our policy to keep the German Supreme Command and Government in Berlin, in view of the change in the war situation, the occasion may arise in which we would move the German Government temporarily to southern Germany."

Almost to the end, and certainly until the Japanese moved out of the Berlin embassy late in April, Purple continued to give the Allied commanders advance notice of enemy intentions in Europe. "Many of us," says Robert Murphy, who had taken part in the Italian armistice preparations and was by 1944 U.S. political adviser on Germany at Eisenhower's headquarters, "grew to rely on the almost daily and intimate knowledge [Purple] provided of the German and Japanese war effort." Then, with the end of the war in Italy and the collapse of resistance in Germany, all interest

General Eisenhower (left) visiting Arlington Hall. William Friedman is at far right.

became concentrated on Japan and how the war there was to be ended.

In Potsdam President Truman met Churchill and Stalin to settle details for the occupation of Germany and to decide the fate of Europe for the rest of the century. And at Potsdam, as Truman was told of the successful nuclear weapon test at Alamagordo, Purple messages between Tokyo and Moscow revealed that the Japanese were putting out peace feelers. It is not certain just how many of these messages, showing Japan's growing reluctance to fight on, passed through Friedman's own hands. But they were numerous enough; and in the years ahead he was often to say: "If only I had had a channel of communication to the President I would have recommended that he did not drop the bomb — since the war would be over within a week."

Chapter Ten

Postwar Problems

FOR MOST MEN in the services, as well as for most civilians attached to them, peace meant the end of the temporary life into which they had volunteered or been dragooned. For all but the exceptional few it meant also an end to inhibiting secrecy. Even for those who had been working on the world's first nuclear weapons, the main secret was now out in the open.

With Friedman, the case was different. The breaking of Purple was revealed in 1946 during the congressional hearings on the Pearl Harbor disaster. But the extent, and success, of both the American and the British cryptologic effort was to remain hidden for the rest of Friedman's life. The reason was adequate enough. Even before the start of the Cold War, the cryptographic services of the major powers were still operating much as they had done through war and peace for many decades, concentrating on potential enemies but interested, also, in what their Allies were doing. Past successes might, if revealed, make future success less likely. Perhaps it would therefore be better to imagine that cryptography had never existed. In any case, that would certainly be easier.

The result was that for Friedman one part of the war went on, not a happy situation for a man whose psychiatric troubles of 1927 had increased to the point of breakdown in 1940 and had driven him to suicidal thoughts more than once during the following years. Now, even more than before, he had reason to question his wisdom in abandoning the pure science of genetics for what was, to a man like himself, in some ways an alien field. And now he began to wonder aloud why he had, as he put it, got mixed up in such a subject; not cryptography, as such, but the mishmash of deception that so often seemed to go with it.

By the late summer of 1945 he was in Europe on official business once more. First he visited Bletchley where the shape of postwar Anglo-U.S. collaboration was already being hammered out, then on to Germany where he advised on the cryptographic organization which would best serve the Occupation Forces. And in Germany he was handed, as a memento, photostats of his own fourteen-lecture course on military codes and ciphers given to American officers in the 1930s. They had been discovered at the German cryptographic headquarters in Burgscheidungen Castle, overrun by the Americans in April, 1945, and had been used there by the Germans for training purposes.

He had also hoped to visit his old friend Boris Hagelin, by this time back in Sweden. Hagelin had remained in the United States until the autumn of 1944, supervising production of the C.38, or the U.S. Army's M.209, as it had become. Then, in the autumn of 1944, he and his wife returned to Sweden, traveling in one of the special ships granted safe-conduct by the United States, Britain, Germany and Sweden.

Friedman's proposed visit to Hagelin had to be postponed until the following year, but perhaps it was as well since he returned to Washington in the autumn with a schedule already overcrowded with work. There were also personal problems. Irreplaceable he might be — and the record suggests that the authorities regarded him as that until he was well into his seventies. He nevertheless knew that some form of retirement would probably come within the next few years. His salary had been adequate but no more, and he began to worry about his finances. Here, it at first appeared, the situation might well change for the better since throughout the previous quarter century he had carried out an immense amount of extracurricular work. From it had come many cryptographic systems and mechanisms which had been patented, although, due to essential secrecy, in such a way that their very great financial potential could not be exploited. It seemed reasonable to suppose, now that the war was over, that the situation could be changed and on September 27, 1945, Friedman took the first step to see whether this was so. It looked simple enough. It was, in fact, to be the start of a complex legal process that was to go on for roughly a decade.

What he now asked for was declassification of a patent he, with Frank Rowlett, had filed in May, 1941, for a cryptographic system involved in the ciphering machine known as M-228. Nothing happened for seven months but, after a reminder, the Intelligence authorities laid down a policy under which such applications could be made. "The policy and conditions under which such an application would receive favourable consideration were so rigid," Friedman later wrote, "that I did not think it useful to submit an application." However, after another year the policy was changed, and he asked for declassification so that he could sell commercial rights in the patent. This was in August, 1947. Three and a half months later he was told it was necessary that "the secrecy order standing against the patent application be maintained."

Friedman now told the authorities that in view of the complexities involved he would like to have legal advice. Would the director of Intelligence, he asked, object if he sought such advice privately; and, if there was objection, would it be possible for him, Friedman, to have the advantage of legal advice from within the Department of the Army?

The Judge Advocate General replied with three points. Friedman had, he stated, been ordered to do the work which resulted in the patents — a curious contention since the Signal Corps Patents Board had specifically allowed him to retain the commercial rights in his inventions even though these could not, for the time being, be made public owing to consideration of secrecy. The judge then went on to deal with the request to ask for legal advice. Here there was difficulty. If Friedman instructed private counsel it could only, presumably, be done by allowing into the secrets of the patents those who were not authorized to know of them. But if it came to involving lawyers employed by the army, there was a more serious objection. Friedman's claim would obviously be against the United States, and Section 109 of the Criminal Code (18 U.S.C. 198) laid it down that any government officer who helped a claim against the United States "shall be fined not more than $5,000 or imprisoned not more than one year, or both."

At this point Friedman, busy reorganizing America's postwar cryptological services, and seeing himself as hamstrung by a bureaucratic machine which had used him for years, became seriously ill. He was more or less out of commission for almost a year — in his own words "from frustration from this and other sources connected with my work and personal situation."

When he recovered, early in 1949, he realized that his request for legal advice had been evaded rather than answered. But on raising the point, he was told that the case was closed. Only with the appointment of a new chief of the Army Signal Agency, as the organization had now become, did he consider it worth while to make yet a further move. This time, the reply was: "The Intelligence Division has no objection to Mr. Friedman's hiring private counsel provided no classified information is revealed thereby."

Once again, from November, 1949 until May, 1950, he broke down under the strain. When he recovered, his first reaction was to employ a firm of Washington lawyers to present his case. They discussed it with the army in June but found, in the autumn of 1950, that the earlier policy had been rescinded in July, an example of outer defenses falling at the first sign of attack.

From this point onwards the case opened out. The authorities admitted, somewhat reluctantly according to the evidence, that Friedman had carried out work beyond the bounds of duty; that while he had filed a number of secret patents, it had been agreed by the army that such filings "include reservations to enable [him] to retain or repossess [his] commercial rights, in whole or in part, if and when the need for secrecy ceases to exist"; and that he had, as a result, suffered financial losses which were estimated by some experts to be as high as a million dollars.

The outcome was a bill which demanded that Friedman should, in equity, be paid a sum of 100,000 dollars since he had "made inventions of the greatest importance, and has retained rights in them which he will probably never be able to exercise in his life-time. . . ."

Throughout the litigation he was hampered by the fact that details of his inventions could not be divulged to his lawyers. He therefore had to write his own brief. The legal tussle ended only in 1956 when the problem was solved by the passage of the bill. He was grateful and not only for himself since, as the chairman of the National Inventors Council said of the bill, it was "a significant recognition of invention as a tool of security which should serve as an incentive to other competent inventors to devote their efforts towards national defense." But Friedman must have had some wry thoughts when contemplating the career of Boris Hagelin, whose inventions were at least on no higher level than his own. Hagelin had, as a Swede, been able to sell these inventions to the United States and had already made a fortune through cryptography.

Throughout this decade of guerrilla warfare with the U.S. financial and legal authorities, the two sides of Friedman's life continued to run in tandem. There was his official work, first as mainstay of the army's cryptographic services, then as chief cryptographic adviser to the newly set up National Security Agency, and finally as the American agent for the Department of Defense on three highly secret missions which ensured America's cryptographic predominance. In addition there was his unremitting study of the subject in its historical context and his purely private work on the great outstanding cryptographic riddles. Together, the two strands were to make up an extraordinarily busy existence.

Of first importance officially, there was the aftermath of a war which had ended with the capture of virtually all enemy material. This involved a searching analysis of what the Japanese, the Germans and the Italians had been doing and a systematic counter-check of how successful the Allies had been. There was also the looming menace of the Russians in the east, and the need to work out with the British the details of postwar collaboration in the face of this threat. An additional and even more compelling preoccupation, particularly after the congressional hearings on the Pearl Harbor disaster, was the need to reorganize and coordinate America's cryptographic and intelligence agencies, a process which was to turn the Signals Agency into first the Army Security Agency, then the Armed Forces Security Agency and finally, in the early 1950s, into the National Security Agency. Friedman was to occupy key posts in all of them — director of communications research in the Army Security Agency, then cryptologic consultant and research consultant to the Armed Forces Security Agency, and finally special assistant to the director of N.S.A.

He was also the best man available for a multitude of ad hoc tasks. One was service as specialist member of a top-secret inter-

Allied board which discussed, among other things, the insecure cryptographic practices of a country which had been America's ally in the war. A decade later Friedman was to be horrified at the defection to Russia of the two British diplomats, Burgess and Maclean; both had attended many meetings of the inter-Allied board. Later still, there came, with the defection of Kim Philby, even more devastating implications. Philby, Friedman knew, had been privy to some of the most closely guarded secrets not only of the wartime British cryptographic headquarters at Bletchley but, through them, to at least some American material.

In 1946 Friedman himself again visited the British cryptographers, now moved to Cheltenham, and helped work out methods of postwar consultation and collaboration. An American Liaison Office was set up in London and schemes were devised for avoiding duplication of effort. Solved material was to be exchanged between the two agencies and, more important, an interchange scheme was started under which men from each agency would work two or three years at the other. The only problem was to ensure that the British should be kept away from American work on breaking British ciphers and that the Americans at Cheltenham should be treated reciprocally.

On his 1946 journey to Europe, Friedman also made a visit to Boris Hagelin at his Swedish factory which was to mark the renewal of their prewar and wartime friendship. "This," Hagelin has written, "was perhaps to some extent based on the fact that we were both born in Russia. But more important was that we were neurotics. Friedman told me once that he had been asked if it were necessary to be insane in order to work with cryptology, and his answer was 'not necessary, but it helps.' The same could be said about me and my penchant for the design of ciphering machines. We both suffered from depressions, but never at the same time — so we could help one another."

In the immediate postwar years, Friedman was involved in many curious operations. They ranged from persuading the American authorities to return to a German professor his very important scientific library, which had been confiscated by U.S. troops in Germany, to the case of "War Secrets of the Ether." This was a three-part account of Germany's interception and cryptological work between 1919 and 1945 written by the German cryptologist Wilhelm F. Fliche. It contained much interesting material, including details of the way in which the Germans had first discovered how to intercept the "scrambled" telephone conversations between Churchill and Roosevelt, and then unscramble the intercepted messages. The United States managed to purchase the manuscript for a relatively small sum and therefore prevent its publication. However, this was only the first step. The book had been secured by the Army Security Agency but was later passed over to the National Security Agency. But the U.S. Government had no wish to pay royalties to the author even though the manuscript was being used. To overcome the possibility required only one simple measure: the document was upgraded to Restricted.

Friedman's work for the United States, both during the war and after it, was on the surface given adequate recognition. In 1944 he had been one of the first two recipients in the whole of the War Department to receive its newly created and highest award, the Commendation for Exceptional Civilian Service. Two years later he received the Medal for Merit, originated by George Washington and the civilian equivalent of the military Distinguished Service Medal. It was awarded, ran the citation signed by President Truman, for "outstanding service conspicuously above the usual" and "for exceptional technical ingenuity which ranks him among the world's foremost authorities." And in 1955, awarded the National Security Medal, he became, with the solitary exception of J. Edgar Hoover, the only person to hold both that and the Medal for Merit.

Public recognition was agreeable. Yet Friedman found it difficult to take at face value his honorable discharge in 1941, his long battle to get money for his patents, and numerous pinpricks from the authorities which grew more irritating as the years passed by. Whether or not he was correct in believing he was singled out for the wrong sort of notice as well as for the right, there is no doubt that the treatment he was receiving combined with the ambiguities of his work were to affect him again. In 1947 he had once more consulted a psychiatrist, this time Dr. Paul Ewerhardt, and asked for advice on what he called "psychic giddiness" which attacked him while walking or playing golf. After some months the treatment appeared to be effective.

Meanwhile, he lightened his official work as best he could, turning with relief and resignation to the delights of civilian cryptography and to the literary curiosities which had a bearing on the subject. One of these was *Gadsby,* a novel published in 1939 and written by Ernest Vincent Wright. Friedman had for long made great efforts to get copies of the book. The intriguing reason was that *Gadsby,* although 50,000 words long, did not contain a single example of the letter "e." The author when writing the book had in fact tied down that letter on his typewriter. Since "e" is the most frequently used letter in the English language, the mere fact that it was possible for a full-length book to be produced without using it had implications for the frequency tables, which are a basic tool of cryptography. After the war, Friedman eventually succeeded in tracking down a copy of *Gadsby.* Then, taking a count of nearly 6,000 letters, he discovered how the absence of the "e" affected the frequency of the other letters in the alphabet — causing him to assume, no doubt, that if one man could write a book with this limitation another might succeed in devising a cipher system along equally unorthodox lines. The differences were as great as he had expected. The letter "o" turned up 649 times in the 6,000 letters as against the usual 447; the letter "a" appeared 587 times compared with 445 expected appearances.

Another subject on the periphery of his career which had always intrigued him was the cult of unintelligibility in literature. "If you are curious to learn why I, a somewhat hard-boiled cryptologist, should be interested in the writings of that cult," he once said, "all I can say is that their writings, so far as I am concerned, are *unintelligible* on their face; that is, they need to be decoded or deciphered (or both) to make them somewhat intelligible; and that anything which is not intelligible after being scrutinised by means of the sieve of cryptanalysis falls within the roving eyes and mind (if any) of the disciplined cryptologist."

What he called his "dilettante efforts to try to make some sense out of modern verse" included a close scrutiny of Gertrude Stein, whose "rose is a rose is a rose" he used more than once in explaining the techniques of cryptanalysis. Naturally enough, he was a devotee of Joyce whose *Finnegans Wake* was for most readers, he said, "wholly unintelligible . . . in fact *in cipher* so far as they are concerned." His opinion of Joyce's writing as cryptographic was, he once went on record as saying, the same as Edmund Wilson's when he wrote: "Today, when we are getting so many books in which the style is perfectly clear but the meaning non-existent or equivocal, it affords a certain satisfaction to read something that looks like nonsense on the surface but underneath makes perfect sense."

Friedman appears never to have fathomed, with any certainty, what that sense was. One reason was perhaps his appreciation that there was in reality a fundamental chasm between the science of cryptography and the art of literature. "I daresay," he wrote to one Joycean enthusiast, "there will be many interpretations (or should they be termed 'decipherments'?) of *Finnegans Wake*. Yours will join those others and it may be as good as or better than most, since you are devoting much thought to Joyce. By the very nature of the case, such interpretations and decipherments cannot be as exact as the decipherments of authentic cryptograms: as [there is] a considerable amount of flexibility in the former [but not in the latter], so that one may get out of Joyce pretty nearly what one oneself finds in Joyce's language and words, depending on one's experience, erudition, analytical powers, patience and so on." And, as he knew well enough, "in cryptanalysis, two wholly different but equally valid solutions is an absurdity."

In the postwar years he also returned to a mystery he had tried to tackle for a brief spell in 1945 as official work slacked off and he found himself controlling a group of experienced cryptographers with little to do during office hours and an appetite for extracurricular work. The opportunity was too good to miss and he had deployed them on a problem that had been exercising him — and much of the cryptographic world — for a quarter of a century. It concerned the Voynich manuscript, "the most mysterious manuscript in the world," as it had been described.

It was in March, 1921, soon after Friedman and his wife had begun work in Washington, that he had received a letter from Colonel Fabyan containing its usual combination of friendliness and command. "Voynich, an old book dealer, has had in his possession a number of years, a manuscript by Roger Bacon," the colonel wrote, "13th century stuff, containing an alleged cipher which is being deciphered by one of the professors at a large University, and whose findings are to be presented in a paper before the American Association of Physicists some time next month. Provided this paper is one-fourth of the importance I am assured it is, it will be given the widest publicity throughout the world by the Press. It is supposed to contain a lot of information as to the sciences, etc. I have been assured of an invitation to this meeting, also an invitation to another meeting where an additional paper is to be read in Philadelphia next month and it was my intention to write you and ask you to attend both of these meetings and give me a report on it."

The professor was William Newbold of the University of Pennsylvania, and the groups he addressed were the College of Physicians and the American Philosophical Society. Friedman attended both, encountering again his former colleague Dr. Manly, by then working as second-in-command in Yardley's Black Chamber, and was immediately intrigued by the riddle of what the world soon knew as the Voynich Manuscript.

The book — for in essence it was this as much as manuscript — consisted of 235 vellum pages, most of them liberally littered with drawings of a botanical nature, with astrological diagrams, realistic or symbolic sketches of living-cell developments, and strange line drawings of nude female figures. All the drawings were surrounded by, and many of the other pages filled with, undeciphered text whose very language was uncertain. It had been purchased in 1912 by a New York rare-book dealer, the late Wilfrid M. Voynich. Although Voynich himself never disclosed where he had bought the manuscript, it was later shown to have come from the Mandragone Monastery in Frascati, near Rome; and chemical treatment of a faded page revealed the signature of Jacobi de Tepenecz, the botanist Jacob, who had been given this title in 1608. It was surmised that the manuscript had found its way to Frascati from the court of the Emperor Rudolph in Prague who had sent it in the hope of decipherment by Athanasius Kircher, a celebrated Jesuit scholar and scientist who had written an early work on ciphers. But in 1912 nothing more was known about the manuscript or the significance of its plants and figures. Voynich believed that Roger Bacon was the author and that the manuscript had been brought to Prague by Dr. John Dee, the famous English mathematician and astrologer known to have owned many hundreds of Bacon's manuscripts. Roger Bacon, not to be confused with the alleged author of Shakespeare, had also written in cipher and it would follow, Voynich claimed, that Bacon would have put down his own theories and ideas in cipher. However, his view was questionable even though, after some years of study, Professor Newbold supported it.

Newbold in fact went a great deal further. He maintained not only that Roger Bacon was the author but that the manuscript clearly showed him to be the possessor of a telescope and a microscope, both inventions which according to history only came into existence some centuries later. In addition, one of the illustrations showed the great spiral nebula in Andromeda, while Newbold also stated that he had deciphered, from the writing, the date of a falling comet shown in one of the illustrations.

Neither Friedman nor Manly, who became equally intrigued with the Voynich riddle, took Newbold's decipherment seriously, Friedman's criticism being based on the familiar cryptographic precept that any valid enciphering system must be capable of producing one decipherment and one only. As he put it in *A Cryptographer Looks at Literature:* "Cryptanalysis is usually and properly considered to be a branch of mathematics and just as the solution of mathematical problems leaves no room for the exercise of intuition, divination, or other mysterious mental powers some people claim to have, so does the solution of a cryptogram leave no room for the exercise of such powers. Two wholly different answers to the same problem in mathematics is an absurdity, when the same kind of mathematics is employed, that is [when] the basic framework is the same. And likewise in cryptanalysis two wholly different but equally valid solutions is an absurdity."

Newbold's solution, however, resulted in just this. Thus a decipherment of thirty-five consecutive letters produced, according to him, the message: "De Via ex Terra ad Coelos. Despicit." Friedman, following the same system, made out of the same letters, the message: "Paris is lured into loving vestal," while his wife, also adopting the same system, produced: "Friedman will uncover secrets soon."

During the 1920s and 1930s Friedman corresponded regularly with Manly on the subject of the Voynich manuscript. Mrs. Voynich had, after the death of her husband, allowed photostats of the manuscript to be made, and in his spare time Friedman worked away on possible solutions as relaxation from the Signal Intelligence Service. On one occasion he applied to one of the wealthy foundations for a grant to fund a serious and major attack on decipherment. But the board of the foundation rejected the application on the grounds that the manuscript would probably contain only trivia and therefore would not advance human knowledge. For Friedman no extraneous reason was necessary. Asked why he persevered, he replied simply: "Because it hasn't been read," a parallel with George Mallory's explanation of why he wanted to climb Mount Everest: "because it is there."

In 1945 the opportunity was particularly great since in addition to the cryptographers he was able to co-opt a number of young specialists in philology, paleography, ancient and medieval languages, and the various sciences which appeared to be discussed in the manuscript. The group met regularly, for one-hourly sessions during which they discussed their latest theories. Some of the basic material was processed by mechanical statistical aids, and before demobilization returned the young men to their universities, a tentative IBM transcript was completed on which scholars would be able to work.

Friedman himself was by this time producing a definite theory about the manuscript. However, always a stickler for correctness, he was, says his wife, "unwilling to disclose it until he [was] ready to demonstrate proof in the form of plaintext which will satisfy the tests, established by professional cryptologists, for validity." All he would say was that the manuscript should be dated more recently than the thirteenth century — probably between 1480 and 1520, a date which ruled out Roger Bacon as author. It was certainly European, the text based upon a written language that could be Latin but might be medieval English, while the "botanical" and largest section of the manuscript was probably herbalistic in character.

The breakup of the Washington group working on Voynich in 1945 was a disappointment. However, Friedman continued to develop his theory and for the next two decades returned to the problem time after time. More than one other body of experts was brought together, the flavor of their deliberations being given by a letter from Friedman to the editor of the *Philological Quarterly* after a 301 computer had become available. "We held the first meeting of 'The Voynich Manuscript Study Group' on September 25 and the next meeting is tomorrow evening, which will be the first technical session," he wrote. "The meeting last week was for background information and both of us gave illustrated talks. Mine followed Elizebeth's and I went up to the brink of disclosing my theory of solution. I wound up with the remark, 'Next week — East Lynne.' There were some young scientists who wondered what that meant."

By this time he was beginning to believe that the basic ideas in the manuscript were indicated by geometrical symbols, modified to express the ideas more specifically by curves, lines, loops or dots. He felt certain that the characters were compounds, but had not been able to find a satisfactory way of separating and analyzing them. Now it was hoped that the computer would help. But before long the computer was needed for other work and, once again, a specialist group intent on solving the Voynich riddle broke up without success.

Friedman's final words on Voynich came some while later, in the 1960s, in a long article he and his wife had written for the *Philological Quarterly*. After he had posted the article, he had an afterthought. "It being a lovely autumn day, and having just finished putting our article in the mail box," he wrote to Curt Zimansky, the editor, "I went to play a round of golf, alone as usual during the week. This is often bad for me because I have not only time to play but also to think. I get ideas for improving (and often ruining instead) this and that, which is bad for one who should be content to leave well enough alone. The idea I have (you've no doubt already divined that I'm about to spring it on you) is this: I'd like to delete the last two sentences of footnote 28 and substitute the following:

> More will be written in a later article about the Margoulmouth and Newbold books; but as to the "Voynich Manuscript," one of the present authors has had for a number of years a new theory to account for its mysteries. But not being fully prepared to present his theory in plain language, and following the precedents of three more illustrious predecessors, he wished to record in brief the substance of his theory: [Here would follow an anagram of some 60–65 letters; if not pressed too much for time I would try to make it a true anagram, as did Galileo, by having it make fair sense in English. Your interested readers may have to deal with their frustrations as best they can; one of them *might* even solve it, who knows?]

If you think this isn't too hare-brained an idea, please reply by return airmail and I'll get busy on this. If you and your colleagues accept this hare-brained idea, I'll ask that you keep quite confidential what is said about the Voynich in our letter to you."

The idea was by no means new, the most famous example being that of Galileo, who, having observed some phases of Venus, believed that the planet would eventually show a full cycle of phases like the moon and would thus upset the Ptolemaic theory of the universe. Galileo felt unable to announce his theory until further observations had been made, but wanted to put his discovery on record without delay. He therefore conveyed it to Giuliano de' Medici in an anagram: "Haec immatura a me iam frustra leguntur O.Y." When his observations were complete he was able to divulge the meaning concealed in the anagram: Cynthiae figuras aemulatur mater anorum — which, with classical flourishes omitted, says that Venus imitates the patterns of the moon.

Zimansky agreed to Friedman's proposal and Friedman sent the anagram containing his view of the manuscript. Then, a perfectionist as always, he sent a second version. This read: "I put no trust in anagrammatic acrostic cyphers, for they are of little real value — a waste — and may prove nothing. — Finis."

After publication in the *Philological Quarterly,* three readers sent in their own solutions to Friedman's anagram:

> William F. Friedman in a feature article arranges to use cryptanalysis to prove he got at that Voynich Manuscript. No?

> This is a trap, not a trot. Actually I can see no apt way of unravelling the rare Voynich Manuscript. For me, defeat is grim.

> To arrive at a solution of the Voynich Manuscript, try these general tactics: a song, a punt, a prayer. William F. Friedman.

The sealed envelope in which Friedman had put his answer to the anagram was opened only after his death. His theory of the riddle was given in the words:

> The Voynich MSS was an early attempt to construct an artificial or universal language of the a priori type. Friedman.

More important than the Voynich manuscript in the Friedmans' extra-service postwar activities was their work on "the Shakespeare ciphers," the alleged ciphers claimed to conceal the real authorship of the plays and to show that Shakespeare, whoever he was, was certainly not Shakespeare. When they left Fabyan and his single-minded support of Mrs. Gallup's pro-Baconian theories in 1920, they had toyed with the idea of devoting a full-scale book to the whole problem, and throughout the interwar years Mrs. Friedman in particular had gone on collecting evidence.

She did not limit herself to the Shakespearean controversy itself but included such fascinating essays as Ronald Knox's "proof," using typical pro-Baconian reasoning, to show that Queen Victoria was the author of Tennyson's "In Memoriam." On the main issue itself, there were suggestions, serious and not so serious, that were just as quirky. "You are a bit late with your thought that 'now if somebody will just write a book proving that Shakespeare was the real author of the Bible, *then* there would be conclusive proof of the cipher theory,' " Friedman wrote to one friend. "For somebody (and we don't know who it was, but this occurred at least half a century ago), pointed out that in the 46th Psalm, the 46th word from the beginning is the word Shake and the 46th word from the end of that Psalm is the word speare. Isn't that quite adequate that Shakespeare was the author of the Bible — at least the King James version? Get out your copy and begin counting if you doubt this fact."

One problem with which the Friedmans had to contend was that the supporters of Baconian authorship, whatever method they used to buttress their theory, were invariably honest; thus they put forward their theories with a dissembling innocence that could at times be disarming. This was compounded by the fact that few of them were sufficiently expert in cryptography to avoid subconsciously twisting their evidence to make it suit a preconceived theory. "Every case that I have examined," Friedman once wrote, "presents clear-cut evidence of self-delusion of a very interesting character. None of these people consciously attempts to perpetrate fraud upon the public or even upon themselves, and it is amazing to see how wishful thinking can distort what might otherwise be fairly normal minds."

Typical was Walter Arensberg who in the 1920s had asked Friedman to lead his Baconian projects. After the war he turned to him again, invited him to California, and proposed that he should head a Francis Bacon Foundation to which he was willing to devote a million dollars. As before, Friedman laid down his own terms — that he would study Francis Bacon's known works, but not search for the proof of a theory. As before, that was not what Arensberg had in mind.

Other Baconian enthusiasts used numerology. The simplest of their systems gave numbers to the twenty-four letter Elizabethan alphabet in a straightforward way, with A being equivalent to 1 and Z to 24, or, in a reverse numbering, A to 24 and Z to 1. To find the number accorded to any name it was merely necessary to work out the total of the individual letters. Bacon thus became equivalent to B(2) plus A(1) plus C(3) plus O(14) plus N(13), a total of 33. Numerous systems were based on this simple method but all were, as Friedman wrote, impotent to establish anything except the gullibility of those who used them. "If anyone still disputes this," he went on, "we shall be content with proving that we ourselves wrote the works of Bacon and Shakespeare. In simple count, 'Wm. Friedman' is represented by 100; therefore, wherever the number appears, as it does frequently, according to the Baconians, (since it also represents 'Francis Bacon') there exists a sign of our authorship. But in case of doubt, we have left additional clues in a different form of signature, 'Wm. & E. Friedman.' " The total here, he pointed out, came to another significant number which buttressed their claim to authorship!

However, such revelations of human credulity failed to impress the enthusiasts and Friedman once pointed out that Walter Arensberg "was not at all impressed by my telling him that I had applied his method to random paragraphs of the Los Angeles Times and had found Baconian claims in them."

By the late 1940s Friedman and his wife decided that they had enough material for a major book on the Shakespeare controversy. Before they could seriously begin work on it, however, he was to pass through another phase of psychiatric illness. Once again, it is not possible to be certain of the real cause; but once again suspicion falls on the underlying ambiguities of professional work — by now much concerned with the problems of genuine postwar collaboration between the wartime Allies — which Friedman was unable to discuss even with the psychiatrist chosen to help resolve his difficulties.

By Christmas, 1949, he was profoundly depressed and entered Mt. Alto Hospital voluntarily but disliked it intensely, partly because he was placed with psychotic patients much sicker than he was. Movement to an open ward from which he could make weekend visits to his home failed to improve matters very much and in March, 1950, he entered the psychiatric unit of George Washington University Hospital for electroshock therapy. "He received a total of 6 electroshock treatments, each without incident or complication," says his psychiatrist. "He made a rapid and dramatic recovery and was discharged from the hospital on April 11. Although he had entered the hospital in a very glum, morose, deeply depressed and potentially suicidal mood, he was almost elated when he was discharged, and in a characteristically effusive way he kissed the nurses goodbye in a rather avuncular fashion. About a month or so later I saw him and his wife at a Toscanini concert at Constitution Hall. He appeared in excellent spirits."

The dangerous corner turned, he now faced the Shakespeare controversy once more. An immense amount of research remained to be done, and it was obvious that much of the work could best be carried out in either the Library of Congress or the Folger Shakespeare Library with its unique collection of First Folios. Regular journeys from their home would take up too much time and they now bought the house on Capitol Hill that Friedman was to occupy for the rest of his life.

It was a town, or row, house built before the Civil War, and almost midway between the two libraries where they were to spend so much of their time. Only twenty-two feet wide but seventy-five feet deep, three stories high and in poor repair, it needed a good deal of restoration before they were finally able to move in during the autumn of 1952. One of Friedman's first acts was to plant a Talisman rose beside the garden door. Since his marriage a third of a century earlier he had celebrated each anniversary by sending his wife Talisman roses — one for each year they had been married. From now onwards a climbing Talisman rose flowered round their door every summer.

Here they set to work, devoting many hours each day to research in the Folger Library or the Library of Congress, checking each of the theories against the First Folio or following the cryptographic byways which the Baconians had opened up. Within three years their researches had developed into a manuscript of one thousand pages, a massive survey which, with no time for revision, they entered for the Folger Shakespeare Library competition of 1955. Two prizes were to be given: one for a book on Elizabethan history and politics and one for a book on Elizabethan literature.

While the judges were considering the entries, Friedman was again sent to Europe, to confer with the British at Cheltenham and to visit the Continent. He was away for five weeks, returned to Washington late in March and spent five busy days in his office and reporting on the results of his visit.

Then, on the morning of April third, 1955, he suffered a heart attack while getting out of bed. He was carried downstairs to the ambulance on a stretcher — past the waiting morning newspaper with its headline: "Washington Couple Win Folger Shakespeare Award."

In the George Washington Hospital it was revealed that Friedman had experienced a major coronary occlusion. The cardiograms showed, moreover, that it was not the first but the second attack, the previous one having taken place a month or two earlier. Recovery was slow; then, in May, there came a third attack. Only two percent of men or women survive three attacks and few doctors in the George Washington would have believed that Friedman was to live for another fourteen active years and to carry out three top secret missions for the United States. "You see," Mrs. Friedman wrote years later, "he was a rare person and made records even in his capacity for survival."

It was early July before he was out of the hospital. He was warned to take life carefully, agreed to give up golf and to walk only short distances, and had to carry with him a supply of nitroglycerine pills, of which he took a number every day. To ease life in the Capitol Hill house the servants' staircase was taken out and a lift installed in its place, while between the front door and his study on the second floor an intercommunication system was put in.

In the reorganized home Friedman settled down, an amalgam of precise correctness and idiosyncrasy. His books were kept in strict order on the shelves and when even a member of the family wanted to read one he insisted, even if the book were not going to leave the house, that it should be signed for. Yet the same man would sometimes come downstairs dressed as usual except for one thing: he would be wearing two or more ties and a quizzical smile. And the two-way intercom not only saved his heart but gave him an innocent delight as he answered the buzzer and demanded the password before letting in even the best-known visitor.

Although on leaving the hospital he had agreed to give up golf, a letter to President Eisenhower in November, 1955, shortly after receiving the National Security Medal, shows that the agreement soon lapsed. "You and I," he wrote, "are both newly indoctrinated members of the ever-more popular 'Coronary Club.' I suffered an occlusion on 3 April, 1955, and perhaps because I was a bit too eager to get back to duty, had another on 13 May. But I am getting along quite well now — in fact, I want to tell you, as one golfer to another, that having recently been permitted to walk around on the golf course and swing a club a bit, I found that my long rest had materially improved my prowess with the seven-iron. I see no reason why the same beneficent effect should not be observable and soon, I hope, in my use of the No. 1 wood and putter."

If there was one essential Friedman lacked, it was a capacity to do nothing, and even in the George Washington Hospital he insisted on being involved in the immediate aftermath of the Folger Award. A number of publishers had asked for the rights of "The Cryptologist Looks at Shakespeare," as the manuscript was then called, and the Friedmans felt bound to give it to the first firm which had asked. This was the Cambridge University Press. However, one problem arose immediately. The firm, although anxious to publish the book, insisted that it be drastically cut.

With Friedman himself ordered to do no work and to worry as little as possible about anything, it was his wife who got down to the task; however, her cutting, pruning and subediting was soon being done under increasingly detailed instructions from her husband in his hospital bed, and by the end of the year the book had been almost halved in length. But it was still not short enough and a desperate remedy was adopted. Two editorial assistants in England read the manuscript cold and were instructed to cut, cut, cut. The result was sent chapter by chapter across the Atlantic and the Friedmans read, agreed or disagreed, as the case might be, and returned the pages. Parts of the book were thus being set while other parts were still being prepared for the printer.

Eventually, on October 4, 1957, *The Shakespearean Ciphers Examined* was published in London. Both Friedman and his wife objected strongly to the title on the ground that it implied there were, indeed, ciphers to be found in Shakespeare, a supposition they effectively repudiated in the book. However, the definitive work on the cryptological side of the great discussion — which the book was acknowledged to be — won acclaim on both sides of the Atlantic and, in 1958, the Fifth Annual Award of the American Shakespeare Festival Theater.

The Shakespearean Ciphers Examined was a remarkable achievement, not only for its cryptological scholarship, which was expected, but for its insights into a complex literary story. It had begun in 1728 when "Captain" Goulding claimed in "An Essay Against Too Much Reading" that Shakespeare, "not being a Scholar," was obliged "to have one of those chuckle-pated Historians for his particular Associate . . . and he maintained him or he might have starv'd upon his History. And when he wanted anything in his Way . . . he sent to him. . . . Then with his natural flowing Wit, he work'd it into all Shapes and Forms, as his beautiful Thoughts directed. The other put it into Grammar. . . ."

The Friedmans dealt with Goulding, and with his successors who had carried on the great controversy. They explained the implications of cryptology as a science and then went on to discuss the various attempts to use it for demonstrating that Shakespeare had not written Shakespeare. They made their position clear at the start. They did not, they said, have any "professional or emotional stake in any particular claim to the authorship of Shakespeare's plays. We have no bias for or against any Elizabethan or Jacobean writer or writers as contenders for the title. It is true that for three and a half centuries most scholars have accepted the attribution to Shakespeare; but it is also true that for a great part of that time the attribution has been challenged by many people on many grounds, and some anti-Stratfordians have been learned and distinguished. The argument has spread to all countries where the plays are known; it cannot be simply dismissed without examination."

The examination ranged from Ignatius Donnelly, the Minnesotan who, before becoming a Baconian and cryptographer, had published two books, one on *Atlantis: The Antediluvian World,* the other *Rognarok: The Age of Fire and Gravel,* two titles on which, as the Friedmans calmly wrote, "the eye of a sceptic could hardly be expected to dwell with enthusiasm." Not all the Baconians were as outrageous as Donnelly, or as optimistic as Dr. Orville Ward Owen, the Detroit physician and one of the first Baconians to be financed by Colonel Fabyan. But none could produce cryptographically plausible evidence for any cipher within the Shakespeare works, not even Mrs. Elizabeth Wells Gallup, for whom the Friedmans had considerable respect and not a little affection.

It was with the account of Mrs. Gallup's efforts to discover a credible biliteral cipher that the authors came to the denouement of their book. The cipher was claimed, it will be remembered, to lie in the use of two different sorts of letters in which the First Folio was printed, one being called the a-type and the other the b-type. Friedman had long suspected that the conditions of Elizabethan printing would have made such a cipher impossible, since what were admitted by Mrs. Gallup to be only minute differences between the alleged "a" forms and "b" forms would be completely submerged in the variations produced by worn or broken type, varied inking, differences produced by different papers and the differing rates at which they took up the ink and then dried.

Colonel Fabyan, as Friedman says, was no fool. He knew that on this one basic point, the weightiest evidence would be produced by a professional typographer. He had therefore commissioned F. W. Goudy, the doyen of American type-designers, to study the types in which the first edition of Bacon's *Novum Organum* had been printed, a book from which Mrs. Gallup had "deciphered" a number of messages. Friedman knew of the commission, although Fabyan had never made Goudy's report available.

However, in the summer of 1954, while Friedman himself had been once again visiting the British cryptographic headquarters at Cheltenham, Elizebeth Friedman made an important discovery in the Library of Congress: nothing less than Goudy's report. With Dr. Gough, she had gone to the Rare Books Room. "[Dr. Gough] rummaged out a huge envelope marked With Col. Friedman and his staff," she wrote to her husband. "Inside it, there was a smaller very heavy envelope labelled: 'Novum Organum' Commissioned but not printed by Col. Fabyan. Also a letter to Goudy from J. A. Powell, Dec. 14, 1919, asking him what he could do for the study of biliteral, both what he [Goudy] could do, and what he would suggest that staff at Riverbank could do. No other correspondence, pasted on cardboard a torn piece of photograph containing your cross-section paper mounting of the capital letter alphabet in 2 forms for the Novum Organum. Drawings of letters in Goudy's hand, also. Then Gough unearthed another huge envelope, this one marked 'Miscellaneous'. In it were two carbon copies of the MS in the Fabyan collection! And you will never guess in a million years what the 'name' under the title, so carefully expunged was, — Plan of the Investigations. Now why on earth would Fabyan have worked so hard at obliterating that?"

But the answer to that question soon became obvious. Goudy pointed out in his report that when type became battered or worn a letter was often "corrected" with a graver, then struck into wax to make a matrix after which further letters would be cast from it. The process would result in a progressive debasement in the quality of the letters and a huge number of minor variations. "Goudy," wrote Friedman after inspecting the long report, went on to say "that some of the italics in the 'Novum Organum' had been in use long before Bacon's time; that some of the variations in letter-forms were due to this makeshift of the printers, and some others simply due to the motly collection of founts all used indiscriminately together." In other words, what Goudy had found was not the two forms — a-type and b-type — needed to validate the biliteral cipher but what Friedman described as a-families of forms and b-families of forms.

This seemed to be a deathblow to the biliteral cipher theory but the Friedmans carried their investigations one step farther. Dr.

F. M. Miller, the F.B.I.'s most experienced document examiner, was given two passages, one from the Prologue to *Troilus and Cressida,* in the Folger Library's copy No. 28 of the First Folio, the other on page 23 of *Novum Organum* in the Harmsworth copy of *Instauratio Magna.* The Friedmans already had Mrs. Gallup's assignments of the letters in these passages to their a- and b-forms, and they now asked Miller whether these were consistent, whether the variations between the two forms were large or small, and whether it was possible to say which letters came from the same matrix.

Dr. Miller's reply, which was supported by many diagrams and drawings, was given in four sentences, which the Friedmans quoted in their book:

> 1. An analysis of the type disclosed the existence of a wide variation among those letters classified as a-font as well as among those classified as b-font.
> 2. No characteristics were found which support the classification into two fonts, such as a-font and b-font.
> 3. Greater similarities were found between individual letters of the different fonts than between various letters within the same font.
> 4. No two letters were found among either of the two fonts which can be identified as having originated from the same matrix.

The findings naturally enough brought down the wrath of the Baconians. The wrath refused to die down and two decades later some Baconians were still stoutly doing their best to discredit not only the Friedmans' work on the Shakespeare ciphers, but even William Friedman's work as an official American cryptographer. His deciphering of Purple, it was seriously asserted, had only been achieved with the help of the British, a suggestion ruled out by chronology if by nothing else.

However, the Friedmans' pro-Stratfordian thesis was supported not only by hard factual evidence but by the almost lofty impartiality of their final words on the subject. "We suggest," they wrote, "that those who do wish to dispute the authorship of the Shakespeare plays should not in future resort to cryptographic evidence, unless they show themselves in some way competent to do so. They must do better than their predecessors. We urge that they should acquaint themselves at least with the basic principles of the subject, and that they conduct their arguments with some standards of rigour. Before they add to the very large corpus of writings on the subject, they might also consider subjecting their findings to the inspection of a professional who has no strong leanings to either side of the dispute. If all this is done, the argument will be raised to a higher plane. There is even the possibility that it would cease altogether."

Chapter Eleven

Secret Missions

PUBLICATION OF *The Shakespearean Ciphers Examined* in the autumn of 1957 quite fortuitously supplied a useful cover for one of the most important secret tasks which William Friedman ever carried out. To understand how this came about it is necessary to recall the changes which took place in America's intelligence and cryptographic organizations following the end of the war. The congressional hearings in 1946 on the Pearl Harbor disaster had reinforced the argument that Friedman, together with many other experts, had been making even before the outbreak of war, that is that intelligence should be gathered, and where necessary deciphered, by some central authority rather than by the separate army and navy organizations, by the State Department, and by other less important agencies. During the war there had been numerous ad hoc arrangements for collaboration, notably that between Friedman and Admiral Wenger, many of which had been given formal shape as the war progressed. They represented, however, only a partial solution to the problem and one of Friedman's main preoccupations in the late 1940s was the working out of something better.

An early step in the complex reorganizations that followed was a tidying up of the administrative situation, and as a routine part of that exercise the Army Security Agency asked the Civil Service for a list of those members of its staff who were already "permanents." Friedman, to the general consternation, was found to be still a "temporary" after twenty-five years, and thus not even properly vetted for the work he had been doing. The result was a special party organized by the agency at which Friedman was tried, found guilty, then formally awarded a medal. On one side was written "To William Friedman for making the intelligible unintelligible and vice versa," on the other, "Presented by those he has led (astray?)." Attached to the medal was the replica of a chamber pot marked The Black Chamber.

The first important change in organization came in 1949 with the creation of the Armed Forces Security Agency, which, as its name implies, was responsible for collecting and disseminating intelligence at the strategic level for all services. So well did the new system work that three years later it was decided to expand the organization into the newly named National Security Agency, the octopus that today handles intelligence and cryptography for virtually all U.S. agencies, that has extended its activities to surveillance of Americans at home and abroad, and has been built into the central agency essential for the running of any police state.

N.S.A. was in its early days the logical outcome of the recommendations which inevitably followed Pearl Harbor. It was set up, however, at a moment when electronics were about to revolutionize not only the possibilities of encipherment by use of the electronic computer, but also the state's ability to eavesdrop on the

231

lives of private citizens. The result was that Friedman, who became special assistant to the agency's director, Lieutenant General Ralph J. Canine, was soon being assailed by moral doubts quite as uncomfortable as those that had worried him when he took over, in the early 1930s, some of the duties of Herbert Yardley's Black Chamber.

From the first, his responsibilities at N.S.A., soon established in a newly built and unbuggable headquarters at Fort George G. Meade, halfway between Washington and Baltimore, were enormously varied. He advised on the best ways of devising new cryptographic systems for special purposes. His intuitive skill as a cryptanalyst was utilized in setting up the teams soon intercepting, and making all-out efforts to break, the postwar systems of both potential enemies and allies. He wrote numerous academic treatises bearing on specific problems, was co-opted onto many ad hoc committees, and remained the essential man to use when everyone else had failed. He also lectured: to the Communications-Electronics School of the USAF Air University at Maxwell Air Force Base, to selected army officers and to students.

Friedman was also the man at N.S.A. who fielded many of the more esoteric ideas which it was suggested might help in the reading of other men's mail. "I have become convinced," went one letter which arrived on his desk "that extra-sensory perception is a reality; that certain individuals possess a highly developed faculty of para-normal perception and, finally, that if one were able successfully to channelize [sic] the talents of those proficient in these skills ('sensitives'), it would be possible to 'see' any document on earth. Physical laws of distance are apparently non-operative in para-normal perceptions. That such a thing is theoretically possible I am completely certain. Whether it is actually feasible at this time I do not know. I am not certain of the present state of research, but I think it an important problem and that the answer might be given by Dr. Rhine of Duke University."

232

Friedman was distinctly cautious. He pointed out that the idea was not new and that "the state of the art (or science) was far from warranting the cost of experiment." He commented on the review of a recent book on Professor Rhine and added: "Much more honest and valid research is needed. I don't think much of Rhine or his results." This last comment was of considerable significance, coming as it did from a man for whom the statistical incidence of what laymen called coincidence had been a companion for many years. His considered opinion, he wrote, was that "until one of the important and wealthy foundations sponsors a very large-scale research project to ascertain the facts and to cast out the chaff from the wheat, not much will be accomplished in this field. I think there *is* something in it, but just what, and to what degree is undemonstrated." And he sagely advised that the N.S.A. should have nothing to do with it.

However, Friedman's skepticism mellowed slightly with the years. In 1958, when the Westinghouse Company announced that it was investigating extrasensory perception, he wrote to the vice-president of the Bell Telephone Laboratories, William O. Baker, asking: "Now why didn't the Bell people succumb to my needling them over the years that ESP is a form of communication. Bell Telephone goes in for studying communications: why not ESP? And now Westinghouse crashes through with a lot of good publicity on a project which, in the words of one recent writer, Professor of Medicine and head of the Department at the University of Virginia, may bring about a revolution of thought greater than was brought about by Copernicus."

The professor was Dr. Ian Stevenson, and, although twenty years later the operative word in his statement remains "may," Friedman was obviously impressed by the need for an objective inquiry which would define, one way or the other, the seriousness with which the subject should be taken. "I won't go so far as to agree with Stevenson," he wrote, "but I do think that there are

233

things there which may have far-reaching effects if they can be established. There of course has been a lot of charlatanism which has greatly blurred the issue, but gradually things are being brought to a focus and I, for one, would welcome any proof that can be established to satisfy my hard-boiled attitude to this whole business."

Far from being hard-boiled, Friedman's attitude to ESP was in fact more open to persuasion than was general at the time. By contrast, it was his reaction to computers, and their uses in cryptanalysis, which lagged considerably behind the current convictions. For a third of a century he had relied not only on technological expertise to solve problems but on an intuitive understanding of the subject. Thus it was natural that he should grant only a circumscribed importance to electronic computers, those logical extensions of the IBM machines he had been so anxious to use in the 1930s. In cryptanalysis they increased, to an almost unbelievable extent, the speed with which a multitude of possible solutions could be tested and no one was more willing to admit this than William Friedman. "The days when hand ciphers were all that were available are gone," he wrote in the 1950s to a man proposing his own out-of-date cipher system. "Automation in cryptography began more than a dozen years ago and I don't think even the smaller or smallest nations today care a fig about them. It would be presumptuous on my part to give you any advice on this subject, nor would I nor could I be of assistance to you in getting *any* Government interested in whatever advantage your system may have — which I don't think it has — over the high-speed, automatic, and very secure systems now in use." But what these systems were quite unable to do, he insisted, was "the thinking required to solve a problem."

As for mechanical translation, a subject with which N.S.A. was soon engrossed, he was even more skeptical. His first experience of large-scale translation had come at the International Telecommunications Conferences at the end of the 1920s. Here he had listened to men who would translate major speeches without written notes and would start doing so as soon as a speaker sat down. He had been immensely impressed and years later commented: "Imagine, if you can, any machine, computer or otherwise, that can or could duplicate *immediately* the feats of such interpreters?" Not that he was averse to experiment. In 1960 he served for a while as consultant to a group studying machine translation systems at Georgetown University, and left only when he decided he was wasting his time. What he did believe was that research and development might be useful in computational linguistics. "I have felt for years," he wrote in 1967, "that *there* lies an area in which properly-conducted R & D might pay informational dividends."

Many makers of the hardware tried to arouse his enthusiasm but his recollections of a visit to the Bell Laboratories in New Jersey suggest that few succeeded. "I have had some first-hand dealings with the outputs of that great great great invention called Mechanical Translation Machines," he wrote. "The latter are assisted by those great great marvellous devices called computers (which make ordinary living nowadays a complete and horrible nightmare). I laughed from my first contact with MT to the very end, but I tried hard to conceal my inward laughter from my VIP hosts, not very successfully, I fear, for dissembling is not one of my accomplishments. Somebody, perhaps you, could gather together some of the most remarkable of these translation bloopers and make a book for insomniacs."

His reaction was not solely due to a clear objective judgment of what was technologically possible. During the last decade and more of his life Friedman became increasingly conservative in his judgments of the world around him. Partly it was the result of a growing feeling that the times had passed him by, partly a reaction to what he saw as, at the very least, the waste and inefficiency of N.S.A., the organization with which the last fifteen years of his life were to be so closely linked. His disillusion with the way things were going, which had begun even before his enrollment as a special adviser to N.S.A., increased with age. It was epitomized in a letter written in 1969 to Roberta Wohlstetter, whose analysis of the Pearl Harbor disaster, *Pearl Harbor: Warning and Decision,* he rightly regarded as the most authoritative verdict that could be given in the light of available documents.

"In my opinion," he said,

> a great deal of the present state of complete disorganisation of all sorts of department store and shop records is attributable to IBM and their copiers — mostly nonsensical and completely nit-wit gadgets for daily affairs. By the way, I know of no case in which "computers" have solved even the simplest kind of a cipher! Think that over. But we have nonillion dollars invested in them at N.S.A. When I was active in the organisation I objected strenuously but the boys then wouldn't listen to this "old fogey." Their use hasn't cut labor costs — they have *increased* them because of the extra work needed to correct errors, made *not* by the computers, but by the *clerks* who have to see to the "inputs" to them. To put it mildly, you would be correct in saying "that guy Friedman doesn't believe in progress." I don't. Too bad! If the progress were in a negative direction I'd be all for it! I don't buy anything that is advertised as "new," "improved," "concentrated," etc. And one of my worries is what on earth are our great Madison Avenue executives going to do when they have completely run out of adjectives such as "new," "new improved," "concentrated," etc. etc. Poor fellows! Maybe our astronauts will find a few new ones on the moon, on Venus, on Saturn, on Mars, or even on Pluto, maybe.

236

The despair which the words betray could be detected early in the 1950s, soon after Friedman had begun to walk through the gates of the newly built Fort George G. Meade. What made the situation doubly ironical was that he, himself, had been among the first to press for a centralized attack on all intelligence and cryptographic problems. At times only a sense of humor enabled him to survive, and it was a satisfied Friedman who for some days walked in and out of the top security areas wearing, on the mandatory identification tab that had to be checked each time, a photo not of himself but of William Shakespeare.

Friedman remained the key figure in N.S.A's cryptographic echelons during its first years of existence, and his heart attacks in 1955 presented General Canine with a major problem. He still desperately needed his colleague's skill; but he knew that to continue employing him once he left the hospital would be a prelude to disaster. "The United States," he commented, "needs Friedman alive, not dead." The solution came by giving him the best of both worlds: a job at home, where a secretary-typist could be assigned him, and a contract, to be renewed annually, which formally required him to produce a series of training lectures but allowed his unique knowledge to be drawn upon when necessary. That settled, he retired from the agency in August, 1955. Two months later, during a special ceremony, Allen Dulles presented him with the National Security Medal for "his many ingenious and extraordinary achievements in a special field of intelligence." It could have been a fitting end to a professional life. However, Friedman was still available for more esoteric tasks than writing training lectures, and one of the most exotic lay only two years ahead.

His heart attacks meant that he was living on borrowed time. Moreover, he had had at least two serious psychiatric breakdowns and his use by the authorities in the autumn of 1957 has only one explanation. No one else could do the job.

The summer of 1957 had been a difficult one for American cryptographers. In the aftermath of the Suez Crisis the British had become increasingly suspicious that the Americans had been reading their service and possibly their diplomatic messages which preceded the Anglo-French invasion. Their suspicions were known to the Americans and it became essential that Allied cooperation and friendship — which on a personal basis had never been ruptured — should be restored at a more formal level. This was not all. Ciphering machines incorporating ingenious variants and improvements were being produced in Europe by more than one manufacturer and were being bought and adapted by more than one NATO country. Thus the awful possibility arose that while the Americans had, before and during Suez, stolen a cryptographic march on the British, the reverse possibility could not be entirely ruled out in the future. So in August Friedman was medically examined, recalled to temporary duty, and ordered to Europe to deal with these niggling little problems.

Mrs. Friedman accompanied him, although she was unaware of his exact mission — so unaware that she later described to their old friend General Corderman how they had flown over from Washington to Europe on August 18 "on a sudden notion, attended to some book matters in England for two weeks, then spent the month of September on the Continent and came back to London October 1st to be in on the birthing of the book." Friedman had, in fact, been briefed for his delicate work earlier in the summer. On August 5 he had been granted a special passport and on August 9 had been formally authorized by the Office of the Secretary of Defense to fly "to Sweden, Switzerland, England and such other places as may be necessary for the successful completion of the mission on temporary duty."

First there was a week in London. Then at 0800 hours on August 26 he formally "re-entered duty status," and was taken by official car to the British Government Communications Centre at Cheltenham, where such old friends as Josh Cooper were still carrying on the work they had previously done in Room 40, in the Foreign Office group of interwar years, and in the wartime GCHQ at Bletchley.

Friedman spent the day in a round of meetings at Cheltenham, stayed the night, spent the next day in a further series of discussions, and only "entered non-duty status" when he arrived back in London early that evening.

On September first, the Friedmans left London for visits to a number of countries on the Continent, arriving back in England only during the last week of the month.

In London there was a day's official work at the Foreign Office's cryptographic office in Mayfair, more discussions at Cheltenham, and then a final day's work in London.

During the intervals the Friedmans visited Oxford and Cambridge, attended the publicity lunches arranged for the launching of *The Shakespearean Ciphers Examined,* and took in a round of London theaters. They might have stayed longer but in mid-October Friedman received an urgent message from Washington: he must be back to attend scientific meetings to be held on the twenty-third and twenty-fourth. "Although we had let no one, not even my sister, know the hour of our arrival in Washington," wrote Mrs. Friedman, "a young man appeared *at the airport* to request my husband to be at the Department of Defense at 10 A.M. the next day."

The details of Friedman's mission are likely to remain secret for the forseeable future, but it is significant that the N.S.A. later stated there was "serious concern" about what might be revealed of Colonel Friedman's missions, since this might deprive N.S.A. of having the daily information enabling the N.S.A. to read clandestinely all NATO countries' messages.

By the time he got back to Washington, Friedman was sixty-six. He had already survived three cardiac occlusions and he was known to be suffering from the strain of work. Yet he was still to

William Friedman caught by a candid camera photographer in Oxford Street, London, while on a top secret mission to Europe in the autumn of 1957.

William and Elizebeth Friedman in their Washington home, 1957. The cipher device Mrs. Friedman points to is an original of the Wheatstone Cipher Device, named for its inventor Sir Charles Wheatstone. Consisting of two eccentric discs — one with 27 characters, one with 26 — it was adapted for field use by the British in World War I under the name Plett's Device.

William Friedman arriving at Frankfurt, April 24, 1958, to visit National Security Agency chiefs in Germany.

be sent, not once more but twice, on similar secret operations.

Before this, however, he was to turn to a literary cryptographic problem which had long intrigued him. This was decipherment of the hieroglyphs used by the Mayas of ancient Mexico, a language which had for decades faced scholars with an apparently insoluble riddle. More than thirty years previously he had written to Fabyan: "A new bug has been itching me for the past year or so. I want to go down to Yucatan, and see if I can't read some of those hitherto indecipherable hieroglyphs. I have been in close touch with the Carnegie Institution of Washington, which is conducting excavations and so on down there. They want me to come in on this work just as soon as things shape themselves properly."

The trip, which was to have been financed by the Institution, fell through, largely due to the demands of Friedman's official work. He had kept his interest, however, and a decade later was telling Dr. Manley: "I have been putting in many hours on the Maya stuff and am not getting anywhere fast. There is so much preliminary work to do before I can really start in to try to read it. Everybody else has merely guessed at it, and that is probably one of the reasons why so little progress has been made other than in regard to the purely calendrical hieroglyphs. You can imagine what a job it is to index hieroglyphs, especially such complicated ones as the Maya." However, he was told by Dr. William Gates of Johns Hopkins University, one of the experts in the field, that if Maya writing was ever to be deciphered it would almost certainly be with the help of a cryptographer. He kept at the problem whenever opportunity offered.

Now, on their return from Europe, he and his wife decided to make the first move in tackling it seriously — a reconnaissance to Yucatan, the northeastern state of Mexico where the Mayan writing can be studied in its purest form. They left in the middle of January, 1958, settled into quarters in Merida, the capital city, and were soon devoting two hours a day to learning Spanish. After that was to come modern Mayan, in preparation for ambitious plans which Friedman outlined to one of his relatives. The following autumn, he said, they hoped to return to Yucatan and spend up to eight months there. If all went well they planned to return each year for the same length of time until the riddle of the Mayas would be solved.

Whether or not they would have finally resolved the problem that scholars have even now only partially unraveled is a moot point; official work and bad health combined to rule out the opportunity.

Less than a month after returning to Washington from Yucatan, Friedman was once more pulled out for a special mission. Once again he was flown to Europe for the Department of Defense. He left Washington in mid-April, first for Frankfurt where he met his old friend Colonel Schukraft, one of the officers who had slept in their uniforms on the eve of Pearl Harbor, and conferred with the head of the National Security Agency in Europe. After that, England, where he met the British from Cheltenham, visited Cambridge to consult with an old cryptographic friend, and spent a day in London discussing with computer technicians from Ferranti, the potential uses in cryptography of their latest machines. He was back in Washington by early May, but had less than a month's rest before he was off again for another fortnight's mission to Europe.

Meanwhile, he reconsidered his own personal future. By the late 1950s Friedman was already disturbed at the trends he saw developing within N.S.A. He had begun to see cryptology denied what he believed was its proper due in the intelligence structure and he felt that he himself had been passed over for less able men. His real roots lay back in Europe. Might it not be best to abandon the United States and spend the rest of his life in some congenial European country. Finally he decided that the United States would remain home for the rest of his life.

For a man who had been at death's door for some years, and who according to the experts would never move very far away from it, his life in his late sixties was still surprisingly full. Describing to a friend the projects that her husband continued to take on one after another, Elizebeth Friedman wrote: "He has been and still is a consultant to the Department of Defense, to the National Academy of Science, to the Georgetown University School of Linguistics; we are constantly urged to write articles, even books, deliver lectures. In fact, life is full of thises and thatses. We are, I am thankful to say, on the whole very fit and well and I am sure we shall die with our boots on."

He himself regretted above all the inroads made by ill health. "Thus far, in my so-called retirement," he wrote to a friend, "I have had precious little time to do the many things I want to do. Much time is taken in visits to the doctor or dentist or oculist, etc. etc. — all with a view to prolonging my stay, more or less intact, on this planet. But I have placed my application for a visit to moon, Mars, Mercury *et al,* so I hope to live long enough to get my visa to those planets. And I hope there will be time left over to look into other things such as the Voynich manuscript and the Ventris-Chadwick decipherment."

Among the "other things" was the historic message sent by Theodore Roosevelt to Admiral Dewey on the eve of the Spanish American War of 1898, a cable which resulted in the United States taking over the Philippines. The encoded message was put on show for the first time in the National Archives and Friedman, naturally intrigued, was allowed by the naval authorities to consult their old code-books. The system used, he found, demanded painfully slow work, since there were three steps for each code group. The first three encoded words in this particular case were WASSERREIF, PAUSATURA and BADANADOS. First, the words had to be found in the code-book and their numbers written down — 99055, 62399 and 11005. Next, the first digit of the second cable-word number was added to the last digit of the first cable-word number, thus turning 99055 into 990556. The six-digit code-group number, 990556, was then looked up in the basic code-book where its meaning was found to be "Secret and Confidential." All of which was, however, only the beginning. The transfer of the first digit, 6, of the second cable-word number had transformed it into 2399; therefore it was not the first but the first two digits of the following number which had to be added to turn it into a six-digit number. This would be 2399 with 11 added on, producing 239911 which in the basic code-book meant ORDER THE SQUADRON. Even Friedman took an hour to decipher and decode the twenty-one-word message, an example he later used to demonstrate that messages should not only be secure but decodable within a reasonable time.

Another of the byways he explored in his retirement concerned the work as a cryptographer of Giovanni Casanova. His old friend Rives Childs — one of the first four men to be trained by the Friedmans at Riverbank in 1917 — had over the years made himself one of the world's greatest experts on the Italian adventurer's exploits. He knew that Casanova had dabbled in cryptography and had collected much fresh material. This was turned over to Friedman who was soon able to show that Casanova, in responding to one particular challenge, had deciphered a document based upon a Vigenère Square, the system devised by the sixteenth-century Frenchman, Blaise de Vigenère. The first such feat had always been attributed to Friedrich Kasiki, the nineteenth-century Prussian officer who helped to revolutionize the art of cryptography. Now Friedman showed that Casanova had performed the feat 106 years earlier.

Chapter Twelve

A Casualty of the Agency

F RIEDMAN'S PAPER on Casanova was his last major contribu-
tion to cryptology. It was also a catalyst which, towards the
last moment of the last hour, enabled him to see in clearer perspec-
tive all the doubts and the frustrations which had developed as his
professional success had increased. Unnecessary secrecy imposed
by ignorant amateurs was one root of his discontent. " 'The authorities' even looked askance at my article on C[asanova] as Cryptologist, thus further making the whole subject of cryptology
anathema to me," he wrote to Rives Childs. "I thought to myself
'to hell with the ignorant S.O.B.'s — have it your own way if you
must.' "

The outburst was no isolated explosion but the culmination of
a long series of disagreements with the National Security Agency

which for more than a decade had frustrated and finally humiliated the man whom the agency itself was openly acclaiming. Many were mere pinpricks, as when he had lectured at the U.S. Marine Corps Schools, Quantico, Virginia, on "Communication Intelligence and Security." The subject was considered so secret that after the event Friedman was not allowed to keep copies of his own lectures. Some disagreement arose from defendable differences of opinion on policy. In the summer of 1958, for instance, he and his wife had attended a SCAMP symposium at the University of California, Los Angeles. The symposium was held in a specially approved, secure, building on the campus, and Friedman was surprised that he was forbidden by N.S.A. from using some of the material he had prepared. However, there may have been reasons for this of which he was unaware: two members of the GCHQ were present from Cheltenham, and the view on inter-Allied cooperation held by Friedman may well have differed from that of the N.S.A.

His own ideas on where to draw the line on secrecy and security were well expounded, after he had signed a year's contract as a consultant with the RAND Corporation. His brief was to undertake "such studies as he and RAND jointly determine to be beneficial to the performance of the USAF Government contract AF 18(600)–1600; such undertakings shall include consultations on the theory of secrecy on the conduct of national defense affairs; methods, procedures and means for establishing and maintaining secrecy; old and new procedures for classifying, handling, storing and safeguarding official documents pertaining to the foregoing matters, and related subjects."

What he had in mind, he said, was the business of "correctly classifying, and incorrectly under-classifying or over-classifying, information to the point where security classification becomes a handicap rather than a help in National Defense." He commented that some old cryptographic material had been upgraded after many years. He found this difficult to understand and he no doubt hoped that his advice would lead to less bizarre situations. Instead, he was to find that cryptographic material dealing with the American Civil War — and even some dealing with the American Revolution — had to be reclassified as Confidential on N.S.A. orders.

The near-pathological passion for security with which the agency began to invest material long open to the world at large became one factor in Friedman's growing disillusion with it, a disillusion which by the mid-1960s spurred him to write: "I am hampered by restrictions which are at these times so intolerable and nonsensical that it is a wonder that I have been able to retain my sanity." The words were not lightly used and there are suggestions that the grotesqueness of some agency actions did in fact drive Friedman to the point of mental breakdown.

The reason for many such actions is plain enough: amateurish incompetence which enraged a man who, for more than forty years, had epitomized the professional cryptologist. For a period, he wrote to Rives Childs, "N.S.A. had as Chief of Staff a major general whose only claim to fame was that his occupational speciality was that of 'mule specialist' (honestly) and the Army by then had very few mules indeed — but a major general of course had to have a job commensurate with his rank. And in such cases soldiers of his rank are more or less automatically shoved into 'Intelligence' — which the guiding lights of the Army and of the War Department thought (and still think) very little of professionally." There was also, he regretted to another correspondent, the case of an assistant director of N.S.A., a transport general who knew only "how to park a giraffe on a train." Yet it would be unfair to imply that ambling inefficiency was alone responsible for the gulf which, from the later 1950s, opened up between the doyen of cryptographers and the agency. On the surface, all was smiles and goodwill. Beneath the surface there was, on his part at least, not only a steadily mounting anxiety, but a self-questioning which at times made him wish he had stuck to genetics, a science which —

in those days at least — seemed to be moving forward only for the common good.

Two factors exacerbated the irritation. One was the political motivation which steadily became more apparent in the agency's actions. Never a particularly political animal, Friedman nevertheless had a basic trust in democratic beliefs and democratic practices. Yardley's Black Chamber had worried him, and he would have questioned his own actions more severely during the 1930s had it not been obvious that the nation was already in the anteroom to war. Throughout the war itself all questionings were overwhelmed by the necessity for victory. Now, as the abuse of telephone tapping, electronic bugging, and a multitude of other systems became more easy, earlier fears began to return. The man who knew most about what was going on was among the least happy.

If this was one factor which tended to cause friction between the two parties, it must be admitted that another was Friedman's occasional lack of deftness in handling the day-to-day incidents in which circumstance embroiled him. Years earlier he had been unreasonably disturbed by a brief and harmless gossip paragraph in an unimportant journal. He had then been in charge of the Army Security Agency and had immediately drafted a letter to the journal's editor asking for assurances that there would be "no further personal articles or references concerning me in any future issues of your publication." Few letters could have drawn more attention to the sender, and when the draft was received by his superiors Friedman was quietly told: "Ignore the article."

Now, with the N.S.A. already coming under fire, his lack of practice in giving the gentle answer that turns away inquiries, came to the fore once again. In September, 1958, he attended an exhibition at the National Archives in Washington to celebrate the birth of President Theodore Roosevelt almost a century earlier. When a local reporter tried to interview him, Friedman stated he was not a free agent. Far from deterring the journalist, the reply led to telephone calls, first to the Pentagon, then to the National Security Agency. The following morning Friedman received a condemnatory call from General John A. Samford, then the agency's director; so condemnatory, in fact, that he responded with his own account of what had happened before concluding: "This letter is to tell you that in view of the fact that I was trying to conduct myself as a member of your team, the tone and tenor of your telephone call to me disturbs and distresses me to the point that I am heartsick that you should have questioned my motives or conduct in the situation." In reply he received a homily in public relations pointing out that he should merely have replied that he didn't want to give an interview or that he wanted time to think it over. "When you make it an official issue, however, the people of the Press can have a gay time just with speculations and can make quite a to do over any official reaction that may be forthcoming," he was told.

This less than happy relationship grew even less happy as Friedman began to realize the implications of a review of cryptographic documents being carried out by the Security Classification Review Board. The treatise on German ciphers used in the First World War, written by his old friend Rives Childs, had been listed in catalogues for years and was readily available on the unclassified shelves of the Library of Congress. Now, the Library was told, the treatise was to be upgraded to "Confidential."

Worse was to come. Some documents had to be classified as "Confidential" because of their "Content," General Samford informed Friedman. Included among them was Friedman's own *The Index of Coincidence,* printed in France in the early 1920s and read freely since then throughout the world.

These decisions could possibly be explained as aberrations by overworked second raters. What followed on the penultimate day of 1958 can be explained only as a deliberate affront designed to humiliate. Three members of the National Security Agency,

Messrs. Reynolds, Cook and Gilliam, called upon Friedman at his home and confiscated forty-eight items from his personal cryptographic collection. Included were *The Index of Coincidence,* many papers dealing with the First World War, and even Friedman's own published paper on the Zimmerman Telegram, which had been declassified in 1953 and had now been reclassified as "Confidential." "The secrecy virus [had] reached its height of virulence" he commented to a friend "and the N.S.A. took away from me everything that some nitwit regarded as being of a classified nature." The only comparable incident had taken place in Britain during the Second World War. Two scientists, one recently naturalized British, the other about to be naturalized, had early in 1940 forwarded to the authorities in London the seminal paper which showed an atomic bomb to be theoretically feasible; it then became so secret that the two men were barred from consulting their own "secret" conclusions.

There was to be an odd sequel to the stripping of Friedman's collection of whatever "some nitwit" regarded as secret. The confiscated material included an article from a 1937 issue of the *Franco-American Review* on "The Restoration of Obliterated Passages and of Secret Writing in Diplomatic Missives." The article is now in the Library of the George C. Marshall Research Foundation with the rest of the Friedman papers, and to it is attached the following note by Mrs. Friedman. "This was stolen from the collection before the latter left Washington. It had always been a favourite of mine to use as a conversation piece. I only missed it after the collection had left and I was looking over [a cataloguer's] list. As you can see, it was originally sent to WFF by Dr. Paul Scheips. This, with two other small items, were returned to me about eight months after the collection was stripped, by a woman employed on the Hill as a consultant to an investigative committee in the House. I knew her only slightly. When I began to question her after she had handed me the envelope, she suddenly had a rush appointment, she said, and fled to the corner of the block to hail a taxi. One wonders what 'obliterated writing' the investigative committee was after that they were driven to steal?"

Friedman's relations with the agency failed to improve with the appointment of a new director in 1960, and late in the year he told a friend that he had just had his first private conference on a security classification matter with the new chief. It was, he wrote, "a shock from which I have not yet recovered. Instead of the possible relaxation in rigidity that had been anticipated in regard to such matters, it looks as though there will be a marked increase in rigidity."

By this time he was becoming increasingly suspicious of the agency's attitude to himself and early in 1961 ordered a private investigation to discover whether the telephone to his own home was being tapped. The fact that no interference was found did little to improve matters and in August he wrote: "As to N.S.A., it is with regret that I have to report that my relations with the new Director are, in the words of a famous or infamous wrongly-translated Pearl Harbor message, 'not in accordance with expectations.' In fact they reached and went over the 'brink of the precipice' last December. It's too long a story to tell — but I think I still have my T/S clearance, although I haven't been in or near the place since then. I am finishing work on my last contract with the agency and will be joyful when it's all done." Shortly afterwards he confided to another old friend: "The N.S.A. considers me their greatest security risk."

And now, towards the end of the day, he could have remembered the last line of that poem which represented the hopes of his parents, sailing west at the end of the previous century.

For I'm the one who left dark Ireland's shore,
And Poland's plain, and England's grassy lea,
And torn from Black Afric's strand I came

> *To build a 'homeland of the free.'*
> *The free.*
> *Who said the free?*

Friedman's attitude was founded on more than the belief that what he called "a deliberate attempt at N.S.A. to block" him was under way. There was, he was convinced, a crucially important failure among those responsible for policy to understand one basic difference between prewar and postwar cryptology. "As I indicated to you in our talk," he wrote, "I think it is a bit late to assume that the degree of secrecy about cryptology of any World War II days can be maintained indefinitely. When we dropped the bomb on Hiroshima, the nature of warfare was changed forever, and when the Pearl Harbor Investigation bomb was dropped, the nature of crypto-warfare was changed forever. I think we should therefore face up to the facts and take cognisance of this one, too; crypto-technology is one of the important weapons of warfare, just as is nuclear technology. Nobody would even dream of attempting to hide the fact that there are such things as nuclear bombs, guided missiles, etc. Why should anybody nowadays think it sensible to try to deny or hide the fact that there are such things as codes and ciphers and that there are ways of making and breaking them — without telling just exactly *how?*"

Yet the attitude did not change. When Friedman delivered a paper on "Shakespeare, Secret Intelligence and Statecraft" to the annual meeting of the American Philosophical Society in Philadelphia in 1962, it "brought frowns in my direction from my superiors," as he put it. He had had the temerity, he wrote to Rives Childs, to mention "certain somewhat shady cryptologic practices engaged in by the British Post Office from the early years of the Tudor period, about 1500 to 1844."

It may not, however, have been only Friedman's references to the British Post Office which worried the N.S.A. He was growing more and more troubled by the implications of the covert intelligence methods whose beginnings in the United States he had watched in Yardley's Black Chamber. He remained scrupulous in refusing to criticize in public the masters whom he served or advised. However, he did not hesitate to raise in unexpected places the awkward questions which he hoped would be noted and studied.

One such place was Philadelphia. His paper was not only a witty piece of literary detective-work but also an invitation to consider some of the serious developments already eating into American life. His subject was Act II, Scene 2, of *The Life of Henry V.* Here Henry's brother, the duke of Bedford, refers to the traitors plotting against Henry's life and comments to the Earl of Westmorland: "The King hath note of all that they intend,/By interception that they dream not of."

"For a number of years," Friedman said, "that scene has fascinated me because it poses a number of questions of some interest to the professional cryptologist." His thesis was that the "interception" was of enciphered letters betraying the treasonable activity of the men involved. Shakespeare makes no reference to this in the play, either direct or oblique, while the chroniclers of Henry's reign, Hall and Holinshed, state merely that Henry was "credibly informed" of the treason. "How or why," asked Friedman, "did [Shakespeare] get the idea that the plot was uncovered by interception? Did his imagination lead him to construct an hypothesis of his own based merely upon the two words 'credibly informed,' as stated by Hall and Holinshed? The thesis of this paper is that that is exactly what Shakespeare did, and I shall try to validate it by a careful scrutiny of Scene 2. Perhaps we shall see how Shakespeare wove the magic of secret intelligence into his *Henry V,* and we may also be able perhaps to offer some conjectures as to why he concocts an hypothesis which was quite tenable in 1599, the year in which the play was first presented, to explain something which occurred almost two centuries before and which authentic history explains in a quite different sense."

For evidence that encipherment was involved, Friedman turned to the confrontation when the king hands the three traitors their "commissions." There has been considerable academic argument as to what these commissions supposedly were. Some of Shakespeare's editors have proposed that they were writs of indictment or warrants for arrest. However, in handing them "those papers," the king first says: "Read them, and know I know your worthiness." Then, as they read, he comments on how their complexions go white — "Look ye, how they change!"

This, according to Friedman, can mean only that the three conspirators have been handed their own enciphered messages, complete with the decipherments that reveal their treason. He buttresses his argument with scholarly comment, leaves little doubt that Shakespeare's audience was supposed to take the point about enciphered messages, even though it is not specifically mentioned, and then goes on to ask why Shakespeare should have written in this particular scene, which is not essential to the plot and has little or nothing to do with the action that precedes or follows it.

Only thirteen years before the play was written the existence of the Babington Plot had been revealed by the decipherment of Mary Stuart's letters which had led to her execution. The rest of Elizabeth's reign had been comparatively peaceful at home, much as Henry V's reign after the discovery of the plot against him had been free from domestic strife. Was Shakespeare, therefore, trying to emphasize the need for the paraphernalia of secret intelligence that then existed, the unsealing, reading and resealing of private correspondence that was then carried out whenever the authorities thought necessary? Friedman does not directly answer the question. Instead, he raises a far more interesting one which suggests at least one reason for his reading the paper at all.

"Did Shakespeare," he asks, "have any private views concerning the ethics of interception, the collection of secret intelligence, and its use in the conduct of public business? I wonder. Did he recognise that it is difficult to reconcile such activities with the democratic ideals of a free and open society that would prefer its government to conduct all its internal or domestic affairs openly, so far as possible, and also to conduct all its external or foreign affairs in the same manner? How far is open conduct of public affairs compatible with the national security of a democracy? What about its conduct in dealings with a closed society? I wonder what Shakespeare's answers to questions such as these might be?"

The questioning of what was ethical in the collection of intelligence material and what was not, was only one of the subjects which continued to worry him. There was another, a subject about which he personally thought it just as improper to make outright criticism — the use made of the huge volume of intelligence finding its way into the N.S.A. headquarters at Fort Meade. A mass of background signals, the "noise" of electronic interception, can often swamp the messages being listened for and it was Friedman's belief that something comparable was happening inside N.S.A. Chary of making political comment, he was yet glad to use, in his paper on Shakespeare and Statecraft, a quotation from the American naval historian Professor Samuel E. Morison. After observing that methods of evaluating intelligence had been greatly improved since the end of World War II, Morison had noted in a *Saturday Evening Post* article on the lessons of Pearl Harbor: "But we were surprised by the North Koreans in 1950, surprised when China entered the war later that year, surprised by the utter failure of the attempt to invade Cuba this year, and surprised by many, fortunately short of war, moves by Khrushchev."

In private correspondence, Friedman was soon adding to the list the unhappy affairs of the U.S.S. *Pueblo* and the U.S.S. *Liberty,* two examples, as he saw them, of leaden-footed inefficiency. "It's Pearl Harbor all over again," he commented. "When will our

257

Armed Forces learn, if ever? It seems that they never learn what's what in present military affairs, only what was what in past military confrontations."

His disillusion with the effectiveness of the Intelligence services continued to grow as did his distrust of the methods they were using. These feelings, usually revealed to only a small circle of friends but none the less bitter for that, were in no sense an indication of any political swing towards the left. Far from it. In the autumn of 1961, when many Americans appeared to be seized with panic at the possibility of war, Friedman wrote to Hagelin, with the permitted bluntness of a Russian-born writing to a Russian-born, a letter disarmingly revealing his opinions.

"There are some very scared people in the U.S. now who are moving out — the deserts of Nevada, etc. seem safe to them from blast — but what would be the use of living in a half-dead world," he said.

Such a letter, also outlining political dangers, shows the extent to which Friedman, by nature an amiable man, was being driven off balance by the treatment of the previous few years and the belief, justified or not, that he had been specifically singled out for harassment. Any doubt is removed by a loose sheet of paper on which he put down, apparently in the early 1960s, some notes of his inner worries. He could not, he said, fully understand his own attitude towards money or cryptologic work. "Have insight into what is wrong, but it doesn't help much," he went on. "My nervousness, depression, at times despondency — frightening to be alone a/c suicidal thoughts — realisation of how wrong that would be in all respects. Flight, fight, or neurosis. For fifty years have struggled with this off and on. Nevertheless have accomplished great deal — my reputation — but feeling of being 'has-been' unendurable. Jealousy of men who have been able to retire & go to other jobs of usefulness and carry on but not I. Why am I driven so by feeling that I must continue to garner laurels. Repression by secrccy restrictions — fear of punishment chimerical but still there. 'Floating anxiety' which attaches itself to anything and everything. Fear that E. dcspises me for being such a weakling. . . . Difficulty re prostatitis? Fear of death? No, fear of living on self-pity. Realisation that my fear of going out is only reflection of psychic feeling of insecurity."

These were the reflections of a mentally sick man, even though Friedman himself may have been only partly aware of the fact. However, during the first days of 1963 he returned to his psychiatrist who found him deeply depressed, with no desire "to go on," and with a complete lack of interest in everything. So bad did his condition become that in February he was admitted to the psychiatric unit of Sibley Memorial Hospital. After four weeks he was discharged. But he was making only slow if steady progress. "It would take several pages to enumerate the ailments that have beset him," Elizebeth Friedman wrote to Rives Childs as he at last began to get better, "the endless examinations, lab. tests, blood and enzyme tests, X-rays, EKGs, the constantly growing list of proscriptions on his activities; his increasing weakness and loss of weight, and after all the pronouncements of what was wrong, the invariable ukase that nothing could be done because of his age and heart condition. He gets 'furioser and furioser' with the medicos, hence finally he has adopted the attitude that, as he puts it, 'the nuts and bolts are falling out,' and that he is going to ignore the situation and do what he feels like doing."

It was hoped that a tour abroad would help, and in April Friedman and his wife set out for Amsterdam, Zurich, and a number of other European capitals. But, except for a few good days in Amsterdam and Menton, he remained depressed and in Zurich even became worse. They arrived back in Washington in September, but it was only after another five weeks in the Sibley Psychiatric Unit that he began to recover.

By this time the root cause of his trouble was becoming apparent to more of his closer friends. "He felt," writes one, "that he had been grossly hurt by the people at N.S.A. because they distrusted him and deliberately reclassified all his papers so that he would not be able to sell any of the historical ones, and he began feeling that the people at N.S.A. were 'out to get him.' "

Disgust at the way his papers had been purloined built up within him even more now that he began to consider seriously the future of his cryptographic collection. He wanted it to be kept together. He wanted it to be available for students of the subject. And if he could dispose of it to a buyer on terms that would provide an economic safety-net for his family, so much the better. The collection contained not only some three thousand books, pamphlets, documents and specialist magazine articles, but hundreds of newspaper cuttings dealing with almost every aspect of cryptography, several filing cabinets of correspondence, manuscripts of his own papers, some fifty complete sets of the Riverbank Publications, a copy of the Voynich manuscript and the working papers the late Father Petersen had compiled in his efforts at decipherment. There were also about fifteen hundred filing cards on which either Friedman or his wife had described the books and papers.

Eventually Friedman concluded that the best home for the unique collection, finally valued at more than fifty thousand dollars, was the George C. Marshall Research Foundation in Lexington, Virginia. He had always been a great admirer both of General Marshall and of General Bradley, then the president of the foundation. Bradley himself visited the Friedmans' home on Capitol Hill when the gift of the collection was first discussed and, coming for twenty minutes, stayed for two hours, so intrigued was he with the story of cryptography which unfolded.

One advantage of bequeathing the collection to the Marshall Library was that it could remain in the house on Capitol Hill as long as it was required there. Another was outlined by Friedman in a letter to Roberta Wohlstetter. "Now *nobody,* nobody at all, will get a nickel out of my estate except my wife, my children, and my grandchildren," he wrote. "Poor Uncle Sam won't get a cent because I will have no estate."

The only thing that now seriously worried him was "the frustration generated by my having chosen as a profession one so enmeshed with measures requiring great secrecy — some quite necessary, some quite absurd or futile — imposed by persons in control of those measures and ignorant of the science, its long background of history, its bibliography, etc. etc." He had, after all, reason enough to feel bitter at the way things had gone. In 1957 and 1958 he had been entrusted with some of the most delicate security work it was possible to contemplate. Ten years later he thought it necessary to record, on February 13, 1968, "Cal told me today records show no 'debriefing' hence, theoretically, I still have my full clearance status." He was, in other words, still to be trusted with his own secrets and those that had sprung from his own ideas.

However, he still found enough to interest him, either in the Library of Congress or in the Folger Library where he continued to follow with glee and skepticism each new attempt to prove that someone other than Shakespeare wrote Shakespeare. Then, quite unexpectedly, he fell ill, was taken to the hospital, and eventually told by the doctor that he had Parkinson's disease. "Having seen one or two victims of that horrible affliction I concluded (privately of course) that death would be preferable," he wrote. "But I am still enough of a scientist to question doctors' diagnoses although I didn't even raise the question with my own medic. I quietly analysed the situation and the symptoms, from which I concluded that they (the medics) were wrong. I merely insisted to my own physician that it would be better if I were taken home. He reluctantly agreed and when he came to see me about 10 days later I *proved* to him that he had been wrong and so had his associates. I made no fuss with him — not once even to crow — but within 2–3 weeks I was all over whatever it was that really upset me

— and I have a good idea about that too. My doctor shook his head in disbelief when he saw me walking and simply said 'Well, I don't understand it at all.' I didn't enlighten him — but he now listens more carefully to what I have to say, because he realises I'm not so dumb, that I'm not a neurotic but a scientist who can think."

He did not have Parkinson's disease. But in May, 1969, he suffered a further serious heart attack which few men would have survived. He not only recovered but did so with a speed which astounded his friends. "He even took charge, as it might be called, of two neighbour-friends," his wife recalled. "One of them was having a difficult emotional time, the other was an extremely brilliant man who had had to retire because of sudden blindness. He made them go for walks with him, as if it were for *his* benefit, and had long philosophical discussions with them."

Once again he began to make plans for the future, and continued making them throughout the summer and early autumn. Then, soon after returning home late on the evening of November 2, he was struck down by yet another heart attack. Within thirty minutes he was dead.

On November 5 he was buried in Arlington National Cemetery with full military honors. More than five years later the National Security Agency's auditorium at Fort George G. Meade was re-named the William F. Friedman Memorial Auditorium and dedicated in his honor. Frank Rowlett, Solomon Kullback and Abraham Sinkov, his first recruits to the re-formed Army Signal Service more than forty years previously, were among those who paid tribute to the man who had helped lead his adopted country around more than one dangerous corner. The higher officials were quite as eulogistic, and, with reason, there remained no vestigial trace of the humiliations which had been inflicted by the agency. After all, it was more than a decade earlier that his library on Capitol Hill had been ransacked; and they had not, as he feared they might, withdrawn his security clearance.

Index